DEVELOPING
DIGITAL
DETECTIVES

Essential Lessons for Discerning
Fact From Fiction in the 'Fake News' Era

Jennifer LaGarde
Darren Hudgins

INTERNATIONAL SOCIETY FOR TECHNOLOGY IN EDUCATION
PORTLAND, OR • ARLINGTON, VA

Developing Digital Detectives
Essential Lessons for Discerning Fact From Fiction in the 'Fake News' Era

Jennifer LaGarde and Darren Hudgins

Senior Director, Books and Journals: *Colin Murcray*
Senior Acquisitions Editor: *Valerie Witte*
Developmental and Copy Editor: *Linda Laflamme*
Proofreader: *Joanna Szabo*
Indexer: *Valerie Haynes Perry*
Book Design and Production: *Mayfly Design*
Cover Design: *Christina DeYoung*

Library of Congress Cataloging-in-Publication Data
Names: LaGarde, Jennifer, author. | Hudgins, Darren, author.
Title: Developing digital detectives : essential lessons for discerning
  fact from fiction in the 'fake news' era / Jennifer LaGarde, Darren
  Hudgins.
Description: First edition. | Portland, OR : International Society for
  Technology in Education, [2021] | Includes bibliographical references.
Identifiers: LCCN 2021026284 (print) | LCCN 2021026285 (ebook) | ISBN
  9781564849052 (paperback) | ISBN 9781564849021 (epub) | ISBN
  9781564849045 (pdf)
Subjects: LCSH: Critical thinking—Study and teaching. | Information
  literacy—Study and teaching. | Educational technology. | Fake news.
Classification: LCC LB1590.3 .L33 2021 (print) | LCC LB1590.3 (ebook) |
  DDC 370.15/2—dc23
LC record available at https://lccn.loc.gov/2021026284
LC ebook record available at https://lccn.loc.gov/2021026285

First Edition
ISBN: 978-1-56484-905-2
Ebook version available

Printed in the United States of America

ISTE® is a registered trademark of the International Society for Technology in Education.

About ISTE

The International Society for Technology in Education (ISTE) is home to a passionate community of global educators who believe in the power of technology to transform teaching and learning, accelerate innovation and solve tough problems in education.

ISTE inspires the creation of solutions and connections that improve opportunities for all learners by delivering: practical guidance, evidence-based professional learning, virtual networks, thought-provoking events and the ISTE Standards. ISTE is also the leading publisher of books focused on technology in education. For more information or to become an ISTE member, visit iste.org. Subscribe to ISTE's YouTube channel and connect with ISTE on Twitter, Facebook and LinkedIn.

Related ISTE Titles

Fact vs. Fiction: Teaching Critical Thinking Skills in the Age of Fake News
By Jennifer LaGarde and Darren Hudgins
iste.org/FactVsFiction

Ethics in a Digital World: Guiding Students Through Society's Biggest Questions
By Kristen Mattson
iste.org/DigEthics

Media Literacy in the K–12 Classroom, Second Edition
By Frank Baker
iste.org/MedLit2E

To see all books available from ISTE, please visit **iste.org/books**

About the Authors

Jennifer LaGarde has spent her entire adult life working in public education. She has served as a classroom teacher, a teacher-librarian, a digital teaching and learning specialist, a district-level support staff member, and a statewide leader as a consultant for both the North Carolina Department of Public Instruction and the Friday Institute for Educational Innovation. A passionate advocate for readers and libraries, Jennifer currently teaches courses focused on emerging literacies and young adult literature at Rutgers University. *Library Journal*, The American Association of School Librarians, *The New York Times*, and the Carnegie Corporation have all recognized Jennifer's work. When she's not busy working, Jennifer spends time reading, hiking, chasing her two dogs, and drinking too much coffee with her husband, David, in Olympia, Washington. Follow Jennifer's adventures at librarygirl.net.

Darren Hudgins is a passionate advocate for creating learning experiences that drive educators of all kinds and their students to think, do, and thrive. He believes in this mission so much that he conceptualized and currently directs Think | Do | Thrive, LLC. Here he uses his more than 20 years in education, edtech, and coaching to inspire critical thinking, champion active learning, and create opportunities for educational communities to improve. As he says, "Let's untangle this world together." Follow Darren at darrenhudgins.com.

Acknowledgments

This book would not have been possible without the support, guidance, and love of many people. The following is an incomplete, but heartfelt, list of people who helped us cross the finish line!

From Jennifer, a huge thanks to:

⚲ My co-author and dear friend Darren Hudgins: I'm so proud of what we create when we put our heads together. You are my ride or die, go-to collaborator, coconspirator, and prognosticator. Whenever I need help folding in the cheese, *YOU* are my first call. Thank you for making my work, my life, and my belief in what's possible so much better and brighter. What's next?

- Ben Kort: Thank you for always being our "beta tester" and for your unwavering pursuit of creating a better world. We are your biggest fans!

- Jarrett Lerner: Thank you for sharing your time and talents with us. We can't wait to see how countless Digital Detectives are inspired by your creativity! Just like your books and art (more info at jarrettlerner.com) your big, generous *heart* is a gift to us and the world. Epic collaboration achievement unlocked!

- John Downs, the Eeyore to my Tigger: Thank you for being a compass by which I can always recalibrate. Your curiosity, news addiction, and fierce advocacy for teachers inspired me throughout this journey in more ways than you know.

- The Lawrence Chaney of librarians ("a legend!"), John Schu: You have no idea how much your endless supply of sunshine and sass kept me going this year. Thank you for being a friend!

- Donalyn Miller: "The Book That Will Never Be Finished" would have lived up to its unofficial title without your tireless encouragement and support. I'm so lucky to call you my friend and sister.

- Brad Gustafson: Our weekly "pre-show therapy sessions" were always just what the doctor ordered! Your friendship and encouragement mean the world to me!

- Rachel Wente-Chaney: The Evidence Locker would not exist (as we know it today) without your wisdom and support. Thank you for helping us find our little corner of the internet.

- Turns out writing a book during a pandemic is hard. These people made it easier: Jeannie Timken, Tim Lauer, Kristin Ziemke, Ryan Redd, Franki Sibberson, Katherine Sokolowski, Teri Lesesne, Cindy Minnich, Michelle Annett, Tara Celustka, Joyce Valenza, Joanna Dunn, and so many others! Your friendship and wisdom have left lasting thumbprints on my heart.

- The team at ISTE, including our editor, Valerie Witte, who we've elected as president of the Team #Jarren Fan Club. Thank you for always believing in us!

- Our copy editor, Linda Laflamme, whose knowledge of '70s-era detective-themed television proved an invaluable resource to us both as writers and as humans! Barney Miller's got nothing on you!
- All the educators out there who are currently on the front lines of the battle against mis-, dis-, and malinformation. Our world needs Digital Detectives. And those Digital Detectives need YOU. Let's do this!

From Darren:

Jennifer, five years ago, we said to each other we would make a big (and scary!) move to write a book to help educators tackle what we then called "fake news." Warp speed through what feels like an eternity, I have the longest hair I've had in my life, the world was literally on fire only to usher in the most challenging year in my Gen X lifetime (pandemic, infodemic, and tribalism, to name a few), and we haven't been in the same physical space in over a year, reduced to nothing more than a personality in a Zoom bottle. Despite this year of discomfort, we managed to put out this book and the Digital Detective's Evidence Locker to hopefully inspire others to tackle mis-, dis-, and malinformation like never before. Thank you for being an inspiration, for actively listening, and for your enthusiastic friendship along the way.

Cheers to solving more mysteries and giving educators the strategies and tools to help students and families solve their own unexpected adventures that will most certainly present themselves in the coming months, weeks, days, and seconds.

To educators reading this book:

In this ever-flowing race to build new technologies and algorithms, create splashy headlines, garner "clicks," and medal in the Personal Value Olympics on social media, we often lose sight of our past. As humans we've taken ideas, remixed them inside us, and ultimately perceived our world differently. Only when we acknowledge the presence of the past can we begin to understand ourselves and the communities we live in. With this in mind, I want to use this acknowledgment platform to thank some people from history whose words remixed my thinking in the development of this book.

"We do not remember days; we remember moments."

—Cesare Pavese, novelist (1908–1950)

"It is the customary fate of new truths, to begin as heresies, and end as superstitions."

—T. H. Huxley, biologist and anthropologist (1825–1895)

"We need more light about each other. Light creates understanding, understanding creates love, love creates patience, and patience creates unity."

—Malcolm X, Muslim minister and human rights activist (1925–1965)

"Writing is for stories to be read, books to be published, poems to be recited, plays to be acted, songs to be sung, newspapers to be shared, letters to be mailed, jokes to be told, notes to be passed, recipes to be cooked, messages to be exchanged, memos to be circulated, announcements to be posted, bills to be collected, posters to be displayed and diaries to be concealed. Writing is for ideas, action, reflection, and experience. It is not for having your ignorance exposed, your sensitivity destroyed, or your ability assessed."

—Frank Smith, psycholinguist and author (1928–2020)

"I'm 38 and for all my faults I have spent most of those 38 years searching determinedly for ideas that work and ideas that help. Not everyone maybe, but some people . . . if they work and if they make any kind of sense, the only way to check is to give them to other people and see if it works. If it helps one or two or ten or fifteen, that's a massive improvement on what most human beings do in their life to help anyone. If it helps a few hundred or a few thousand, that's incredible."

—Genesis P-Orridge, singer-songwriter, musician, poet, performance artist, visual artist, and occultist (1950–2020)

"The economics of social media favor gossip, novelty, speed, and 'shareability.'"

—Simeon Yates, associate pro-vice-chancellor and former professor (present)

"Part of our contemporary crisis is created by a lack of meaningful access to truth. That is to say, individuals are not just presented untruths but are told them in a manner that enables the most effective communication. When this collective cultural consumption of and attachment to misinformation is coupled with the layers of lying individuals do in their personal lives, our capacity to face reality is severely diminished as is our will to intervene and change unjust circumstances."

—bell hooks (the pen of Gloria Jean Watkins), author, professor, feminist, and social activist (1952–present)

Publisher's acknowledgments

ISTE gratefully acknowledges the contributions of the following:

ISTE Standards reviewer

Austin Moore

Manuscript reviewers

Jacqueline Liesch

Mary Townsend

Kathy Schmidt

Evelyn Wassel

Susan Grigsby

Heather Lister

Dedication

To David: I'd be lost without you. Xoxo—Candy

To Dr. Ken Bort, Ph.D.: In a world full of fakes, you're the real deal.

—Jennifer

To all those who asked us to answer the call after Fact vs. Fiction: *Psst . . . now join our #digitaldetectivesquad.*

To my family who had to endure the car rides, TV viewing, and information consumption where I shouted sarcastically, "Fiction can be fun!"

—Darren

Contents

Introduction

Let's Get Started!

 A variety of resources related to this chapter can be found in the Digital Detective's Evidence Locker. Use the QR code to the left, or visit evidencelocker.online. Then navigate to Introduction.

> The recent weeks and months have taught us a painful lesson. There is truth and there are lies, lies told for power and for profit. And each of us has a duty and a responsibility as citizens, as Americans, and especially as leaders . . . to defend the truth and defeat the lies.
>
> —U.S. President Joseph R. Biden

On January 6, 2021, a group of rioters, some of whom were armed, forced their way into the United States Capitol in Washington, D.C. Millions of people around the world, including perhaps some of the demonstrators in Washington who were there to protest the outcome of the 2020 presidential election, watched in shock as the mob overtook the Capitol Police, scaled barricades, and swarmed the steps, until finally breaking through locked windows and doors to storm the seat of American democracy. While their ultimate goal of confronting and even harming specific lawmakers (such as the Vice President of the United States) was unsuccessful, a number of people were killed and many others were injured.

As these events unfolded, the world was facing a series of other unprecedented crises: a global pandemic and the resulting infodemic (WHO et al., 2020), climate change, and an ongoing struggle for racial justice (to name just a few). All of these monumental challenges have one thing in common: They are all fueled, and worsened, by misinformation, disinformation, and malinformation.

Just as the events of January 6, 2020 were spurred on by conspiracy theories about the recent presidential election, global efforts to address COVID-19, climate change, and racial injustice have been hampered by social media–fueled disinformation and entrenched group thinking. It's for this reason that we believe mis-, dis-, and malinformation, and their effect on the decisions we make, are the greatest threats facing our world today. If that sounds hyperbolic, we assure you that it isn't. Until we get a handle on our own ability to determine what can and can't be trusted in the information we consume, we stand very little chance of truly confronting the other problems we face as a species.

There's an old saying that goes, "The definition of insanity is repeating the same actions and expecting different results." Information literacy is not a new discipline. And yet, traditional approaches to this work are clearly not cutting it. In light of all the challenges we face, we believe that continuing to apply the same methods to this problem, while keeping our fingers crossed for better outcomes, not only fits this definition of insanity but is also incredibly irresponsible. Today's complex information landscape requires learners of all ages to be *Digital Detectives*: information sleuths who actively pursue clues to credibility by examining information through multiple lenses.

The Four Lenses

This book comprises, essentially, two sections. Chapters 1 through 4 describe the protocol we've developed for evaluating false information: the Four

Lenses. Unlike traditional checklists that ask learners to seek and find a static, right answer to the question of whether content can be trusted, the Four Lenses magnify the connection between our own emotional responses to information and our ability to thrive during an infodemic. The Four Lenses are a tool for understanding and evaluating the relationship between the motives of those who create and spread false content and what we bring to the table as human beings. With that in mind, no single lens represents a "Go Directly to Jail" card: a one-and-done tool for identifying what can be trusted from what can't. Taken together and in order, the Four Lenses are a nuanced approach to information literacy that challenges learners to think deeply about the information they consume, how that information affects them, and how their behavior online affects others and our world.

1. The **Triggers Lens** (Chapter 1) helps Digital Detectives recognize how information is designed to trigger an emotional response and how those responses then drive our behavior online. More importantly, however, this lens supports educators in the work of helping learners develop strategies for managing those triggers so that they are better able to navigate and evaluate the information they consume.

2. The **Access Lens** (Chapter 2) helps learners understand how the device through which they are accessing information influences their ability to determine what can be trusted. In addition to the layers social media adds to the process of locating traditional markers of credibility, the Community Reading Experience, which accompanies content shared in those spaces, plays a role in influencing our decisions as content creators and consumers. The Access Lens allows Digital Detectives to take control of their device, rather than letting the device control them.

3. The **Forensics Lens** (Chapter 3) supports Digital Detectives in the work of developing authentic investigations to guide their searches for credibility clues. Long gone are the days when a simple checklist or mnemonic device was sufficient to the task of determining whether information can be trusted. This lens seeks to help learners develop the skills for creating the

targeted, curiosity-fueled investigations that are an essential component of this work.

4. The **Motives Lens** (Chapter 4) helps learners step inside the shoes of both the bad actors who intentionally create and spread malinformation online and those who unwittingly pass on that false content to their own networks and friends lists. Understanding the motives that fuel those actions help Digital Detectives recognize the tools and tricks that are commonly used to get the job done.

While the first four chapters unpack the reasoning behind each lens, they also provide guidance for how to understand and use them. Each of these chapters also contains resources and mini-lessons for supporting students as they begin the work of the Digital Detective. Ultimately, this book is about looking at information literacy in a new way. In the chapters that follow, we're going to challenge the way this work has always been done, but more importantly, we're going to give you the strategies and resources for doing things differently.

The Four Lenses in Action

The second part of this book is made up of unit plans or "cases" for Digital Detectives to solve. These unit plans are organized by grade span and are supported by tools and resources to help you implement them as soon as you feel your Digital Detectives are ready to start cracking cases. In addition, we've listed the relevant indicators of both the ISTE Standards for Students and the ISTE Standards for Educators in each unit to help you align our unit plans with the Standards.

We recognize that connecting information literacy to robust instructional standards is important. With that in mind, the ISTE Standards for Students emphasize the skills and qualities needed to help learners engage and thrive in a connected, digital world. Scan the QR code or visit iste.org/standards/for-students to view the ISTE Standards for Students in full.

The ISTE Standards for Educators naturally support the task of developing Digital Detectives. These standards can deepen your understanding of how this work relates to other digital age pedagogical practices, while also providing pathways for collaboration with peers. Scan the QR code or visit iste.org/standards/for-educators to view the ISTE Standards for Educators in full.

Exploring the Digital Detective's Evidence Locker

Both sections of the book are aligned with and supported by an online resource we've called the **Digital Detective's Evidence Locker**. Think of the Evidence Locker as a hybrid between the "teacher's edition" of a traditional textbook and a carefully curated resource repository. Although you'll no doubt share many of the resources there with learners, ultimately the Evidence Locker itself was designed for educator use.

You'll find well over 100 resources linked in the **Digital Detective's Evidence Locker**, and our goal is to continue adding to and updating them over time. What's more, because all the resources and tools related to this book are housed in one spot, you'll only ever have to go to one link for everything you need to implement the ideas you read about here! The link for the Evidence Locker, along with a QR code for easy digital access, can be found at the beginning of each chapter, and throughout the chapters, visual cues (as in the margin here) provide reminders to check the **Digital Detective's Evidence Locker** for useful resources. Together, the book you're reading and the Evidence Locker reflect nearly two years of work and comprise what we believe (and hope!) will become a rich and robust resource to support the work of helping your learners develop into Digital Detectives.

A Word About *Fact vs. Fiction*

If you haven't read our first book, *Fact vs. Fiction: Teaching Critical Thinking Skills in the Age of Fake News*, don't worry. That text is not a prequel to this one. However, there are some connections between both books that we want to briefly address.

Our primary goals in *Fact vs. Fiction* were to:

- Create a sense of urgency around the need to address information literacy in K–12 education
- Point educators toward what were, at the time, the best available resources for getting started

While we shared numerous activities and mini-lessons in that book, we were careful not to prescribe a single approach, leaving it up to educators in the field to select the best strategies for their learners.

In the months that followed the publication of that book, as we continued to work with educators to craft lessons and curricula for helping kids parse fact from fiction in the information they consume, our thinking evolved in ways that made a second book about Digital Detective work feel necessary. For example, in *Fact vs. Fiction*, we made (what we think is) a strong case for including mobile devices in all information literacy instruction. In this book, we'll take that argument to the next level by connecting our original ideas to social-emotional learning (SEL). While tools and technology both change rapidly, human behavior is remarkably predictable. With that in mind, we've underpinned all Four Lenses with a foundation based on how emotion affects our ability to determine what can be trusted. The Triggers Lens takes the deepest dive into that thinking; however, all Four Lenses are informed by what we bring to the table as social and emotional creatures.

Similarly, in *Fact vs. Fiction* we maintained that technology wasn't the cause of disinformation but was rather its enabler and amplifier. In this book, we build on that idea by focusing on the neuroscience that causes us to fall for false content and how we can help learners recognize when they are being driven by emotion rather than logic.

One major difference you'll notice between our first book and the second is that while the term "fake news" appears in both titles, we intentionally included quotation marks around it in this one. In our first book, we encouraged educators to be more specific when describing false content online, challenging them to identify the specific type of misleading information being shared, such as conspiracy theory or manipulated statistics. In this book, we're following our own advice, but more importantly, we've also come to believe that the term fake news itself has become toxic: a slur sometimes used to discredit content that challenges one's own beliefs. That's why, apart from this in explanation (and the title), the term doesn't appear anywhere else in this book.

This We Believe

Finally, before we get started, we want to share the core beliefs that underpin this book:

- **Facts matter.** The prevalence of mis-, dis-, and malinformation online makes it tempting to think that nothing can be trusted, but that is false. Facts are everywhere; it's up to us to detect and amplify them.

- **There may be two sides to every story, but not every side has earned the right of critical debate.** Only arguments based in facts warrant merit. For example, the Earth is round. This is a fact we've known for over 2,000 years. (Hogenboom, 2016). Although some people believe the Earth is flat, those beliefs are based in conspiracy theory and junk science. Giving equal debate time to conspiracy theories only lends them credibility they do not deserve.

- **Disinformation is a human problem.** The tangled digital disinformation mess we find ourselves in right now is a result of human error. We're not facing an unnamed, unknowable nemesis. The problem is within us—which means, so is the solution.

- **Our world needs Digital Detectives.** Despite the perception that we are more divided and fractured than ever, there are some things we can and must agree on: The challenges we face as a species are monumental. The consequences for inaction are dire. We may not always agree on who is to blame or who has the best solution, but we do know that the answers to those questions must be rooted in facts. The stakes have never been higher. Let's get started!

The First Lens: Triggers

Reminder: A variety of resources related to this chapter can be found in the **Digital Detective's Evidence Locker**. Use the QR code to the left, or visit evidencelocker.online, then navigate to Chapter 1.

> Even when the researchers controlled for every difference between the accounts originating rumors—like whether that person had more followers or was verified—falsehoods were still 70 percent more likely to get retweeted than accurate news. [Additionally] content that arouses strong emotions spreads further, faster, more deeply, and more broadly.
>
> —Soroush Vosoughi, Deb Roy, and Sinan Aral

Explore This Lens

We all know what it's like to read, watch, or hear something online that evokes an extreme emotional reaction. Before we know it, we're tapping out a strongly worded, 240-character editorial to post alongside it when we pass the same content on to our own network of followers. Although the emotions involved often feel complicated and difficult to untangle, the chain of events that begins when we encounter an **emotional trigger** and ends with us liking and/or sharing information that we haven't fully vetted is really quite simple.

Our brains are remarkably good at classifying information. This is a product of evolutionary efficiency. Let's use the book you're reading as an example. Whether you're reading a physical or digital copy, or you're listening to this as an audiobook, your brain didn't have to spend time analyzing what it was encountering. Your brain already knows what a book is. It didn't have to exert any energy deciding whether or not the book was dangerous. Your brain didn't have to figure out the book's function. Your brain has already classified what a book is, so that analysis isn't necessary. With these tasks handled automatically in milliseconds, your brain could focus on other tasks, including the work of interpreting and applying the book's content. In *Fact vs. Fiction: Teaching Critical Thinking Skills in the Age of Fake News*, we unpacked the concept of confirmation bias, or the idea that once we've established an opinion about something, we dismiss any information that contradicts those beliefs. In his book *Talking to Strangers: What We Should Know about the People We Don't Know* (2019), Malcolm Gladwell highlighted the work of Timothy R. Levine, who calls this phenomenon "defaulting to truth," with *truth* meaning anything that our brains have already classified into the category of representing truth.

Let's look at the example of *Developing Digital Detectives* again. If you picked up this book assuming it would be great, because of its reviews or your prior experience with the authors, it would take a lot of evidence to make you think otherwise. You might have even initially dismissed contradictory evidence because your brain had already made some decisions about what was true about the book. This may be a demonstration of confirmation bias because the new information about the book contradicts your already existing beliefs. But it could also be an example of *ambiguity aversion*, which refers to our brain's default toward known information versus that which is unknown. As the old saying goes, "better the devil you know than the one you don't." In this example, it's likely that you would dismiss new knowledge about the book because the known information requires less work for your brain to process. Our brains prefer the ease of autoprocessing already known content to the cognitive workout required in analyzing the unfamiliar. Obviously, we hope you love our book, but as Gladwell pointed out, when it comes to media literacy, our brains are often working against us. "Defaulting to truth is a problem," he stated. "It lets spies and con artists roam free" (2019, p. 93). Gladwell posited that rather than defaulting to truth, we need to retrain our brains to default to skepticism. But flipping this switch isn't as easy as it sounds.

Fight-or-Flight Response

When our brains encounter something unfamiliar or potentially dangerous, we quickly pivot to **fight-or-flight response**, in which all of our mental (and sometimes physical) energy is devoted to addressing the perceived threat. Researchers at Harvard Medical School have done extensive research into this response and found that when faced with information that feels unknown or threatening, our brains send out a distress signal to the rest of the body through the autonomic nervous system, "which controls such involuntary body functions as breathing, blood pressure, heartbeat, and the dilation or constriction of key blood vessels and small airways" (Harvard Health Publishing, 2020). These physical responses can be uncomfortable or even painful, but more importantly they then trigger emotions that end up guiding our decision-making. We all know what it's like to shake our heads and think, "I'd be so much smarter than that," while watching the main character in a horror movie make a bafflingly terrible decision in the face of extreme danger. Chances are, however, we wouldn't be smarter. In fight-or-flight mode, the part of our brain that takes over is only horror-movie-level smart, which isn't very smart at all.

Emotion in the Driver's Seat

But it's not just fear that can push our brains into fight-or-flight mode and trigger a stress response. Other emotions can do the trick, too. Sometimes referred to as the "Big Seven," the emotions of fear, anger, greed, superiority, envy, and guilt, as well as the sense of belonging are profoundly effective at driving our decisions. Professional marketers have known for years that triggering an emotional response is the most effective way to get people to buy (Oetting, 2017).

In marketing, the acronym AIDA refers to the different phases through which a consumer goes before buying a product or service (Figure 1.1). Although coined in the late 1800s, this model of consumer attraction is still widely used today.

	Marketing	News/Information
A	**Attention**: Image, color, layout, typography, size, celebrity, model, and so on are used to grab attention.	Journalists and other content creators also use headlines, ledes, chyrons, bylines, and/or photo and video captions to do the important work of capturing our attention.
I	**Interest**: Once attention is grabbed, it's necessary to create interest in the viewer's mind so that they will read more about the brand being advertised. Interest can be invoked through the use of an attractive subhead.	In the digital world, the Community Reading Experience, which includes likes and share counts alongside comments from other users, also drives interest. The platforms where the most news/information is shared often prioritize these elements by featuring comments that receive the most interaction or by pointing us to what's "trending."
D	**Desire**: Body copy describing in detail the necessity of buying the product or service can explain the features of the brand and offer key facts and figures, thereby creating the element of desire.	In a click-driven information landscape, all content creators want theirs to be the stories, videos, and posts that go viral. This makes the desire to like, share, or comment the most important urge any form of information can inspire. Triggering extreme emotion has proven an effective way to ensure that this happens.
A	**Action:** Contact information for the brand is provided in a convenient place to encourage customers to take action immediately. This can be in the form of a shop address, toll-free numbers, or a website address.	While marketers need us to take action to purchase, journalists and other content creators need us to *interact* with information. Our clicks result in revenue. The more we click, the more money is generated. And the more extreme the emotion a story, photo, or video evokes, the more likely we are to click.

Figure 1.1 AIDA model of consumer attraction applied to news creation

AIDA's focus on emotion as a driver can be applied to how news and information is produced in the digital age and should profoundly affect how we approach information literacy. For marketers and other sales people, the goal is for us to make a purchase. But what happens when WE, our engagement, our time and attention, our browsing histories and patterns, our personal data, our affiliations, our ideologies and personal identities, are the product being sold?

The High Price of Free Information

Whether you picture a physical partition to prevent flames from spreading in the event of a fire or software designed to block unauthorized access and keep users from unsafe content, the word **firewall** calls to mind a barrier. Safety lies on one side and potential danger on the other. For years, journalism had its own version of a firewall. If not a physical barrier, a philosophical one kept the content of the news separated from the business of raising revenue through advertising and the danger of being biased by money's influence. In some institutions, reporters worked in a separate area from other employees who sold the ads that appeared alongside content or the subscriptions that funded the entire operation. But in most cases, the firewall was metaphorical: an ideology that prevented the need for revenue from influencing how the news was reported. As Ira Basen noted in his essay "Breaking Down the Wall" (2012), "From the start, there has been a strong whiff of mythology about the separation between the business office and the newsroom, but rhetorically at least, the idea that editorial decisions would be made independent of the wishes of advertisers has long been considered to be one of journalism's most fundamental principles."

In 2013, however, *Time* became the first major news outlet to "abandon the traditional separation between its newsroom and business sides" in order to remain solvent (Haughney, 2013). This razing of the firewall at *Time* was as shocking as it was predictable. While the internet has (to some degree) democratized access to information, that shift has not come without consequences. According to the Pew Research Center, newsroom employment at U.S. newspapers has dropped by nearly half since 2008. This reduction in force reflects a jarring 62% drop in ad revenue during the same time period (Grieco, 2020). Other news platforms haven't fared much better in an environment in which subscription models are dead and clicks are the new currency. Today, journalists and their editors no longer have the luxury of the firewall. Like every other person creating information on the internet, those publications that have managed to survive must take steps to ensure that theirs are the stories, videos, and posts that go viral.

We now expect information to be free. We no longer subscribe to newspapers in large numbers, and we've all become experts at bypassing paywalls, but we still pay: through our clicks. Just as marketers understand that emotion is the key to sales, today's information creators know that one incredibly effective strategy for increasing engagement with online content is to embed **emotional triggers** at every access point. This is where those Big Seven emotions come into play. A 2018 study from MIT found that "content that arouses strong emotions spreads further, faster, more deeply, and more broadly online" (Meyer, 2018). Peppering headlines, bylines, sidebars, and even photo captions with words that elicit an extreme emotional response and/or confirm existing biases helps to increase the likelihood that a story, video, or post will be clicked, liked, and shared. When we connect with news that triggers an extreme emotion like fear, anger, or outrage, our immediate urge is to express that emotion—often by passing on the information (along with our feelings about it) to others. Too often, however, this happens without fact-checking or, in some cases, even reading the entire article.

A 2015 study found that as our access to information increases, the ability to hold our attention declines, concluding: "Heavy multi-screeners find it difficult to filter out irrelevant stimuli—they're more easily distracted by multiple streams of media" (McSpadden, 2015). The same study estimated that on average, people lose the ability to concentrate on information after about eight seconds. This gives the creators of that content a very small window to not only grab your attention but also connect you with an emotional trigger that makes you want to like or share their work. Once the emotion is driving, all our background knowledge about how to parse credibility flies out the window. Creators and spreaders of disinformation count on this reaction. Chances are, if I'm outraged by a news story and I share it, others in my network will also be outraged and pass it on to their networks, who will then share with theirs . . . and so on and so forth.

The death of the firewall has forever changed journalism as we know it. As *Los Angeles Times* reporter David Shaw wrote,

> A wall has its flaws; it's hard to see over it or talk through it, and that's not conducive to the kind of communication and cooperation so vital to the survival of newspapers today. But a wall is also impregnable and immovable, at least in theory; a line can be breached much more easily, moved so gradually that no one knows it has actually been moved until it's too late, and principles have been irrevocably compromised. (as quoted in Basen, 2012)

And yet, information literacy instruction has, largely, not kept pace. We can't roll back the clock to a time when information wasn't so heavily influenced by revenue, but we can work to evolve our instruction so that it is relevant in a post-firewall world.

Teach This Lens: Triggers

The way our brains process and respond to information is why traditional approaches to news and media literacy are insufficient. Even though we've been taught to seek out more information about a source or read laterally to confirm claims, those skills become impossible to employ when our brains have been hijacked by an extreme emotion. We believe that by failing to arm learners with the tools for recognizing and managing their emotional response to information, we've left them unprepared for the work of detecting other credibility clues.

This is why the first lens through which Digital Detectives must examine information is the Triggers Lens. This lens requires Digital Detectives to first think about how information makes them feel. Before trusting, sharing, or otherwise endorsing information they find online, Digital Detectives must first ask themselves a series of questions:

1. How does this information make me feel?
2. Even if this information does not trigger me, are there elements that might be triggering to others?
3. How do the feelings from the previous two questions affect my urge to trust or share this information?

The answers to these questions can be credibility red flags, and Digital Detectives must learn to look at them as clues. (Check the **Digital Detective's Evidence Locker** for an infographic to help students understand the questions that define the Triggers Lens.) But these foundational questions are really only the beginning of what this lens pushes Digital Detectives to do. Ultimately, the Triggers Lens should also help Digital Detectives think deeply about how emotional triggers may influence the behavior of others and what responsibility they have to consider this as information consumers, creators, and members of information-rich communities.

Information Literacy + Social-Emotional Learning = Vital Combination

In the two years since *Fact vs. Fiction* came out, we've worked with countless educators around the country to help them create learning opportunities for students that better prepare them for our complex news and information landscape. That work illuminated several things for us, one of the most important being that there is an inextricable, and yet largely untapped, link between information literacy and social-emotional learning (SEL), or the "process through which children and adults understand and manage emotions, set and achieve positive goals, feel and show empathy for others, establish and maintain positive relationships, and make responsible decisions" (CASEL, 2020). What's more, we believe this gap is at the heart of why so many information literacy efforts fail.

We know that news is designed to trigger an emotional response. And yet, teaching kids to recognize and manage those triggers is not a component of most of the news and information literacy protocols that we encounter. While many schools are looking for ways to incorporate news literacy and SEL into curricula individually, we believe that the relationship between news and emotion creates an opportunity for them to be combined. The Collaborative for Academic, Social, and Emotional Learning (CASEL) has established a framework for understanding SEL that revolves around five core competencies. These competencies fall into three broad categories: self-awareness, social awareness, and responsible decision-making, which mirror the three questions that underpin the Triggers Lens:

1. How does this information make me feel?
2. Even if this information does not trigger me, are there elements that might be triggering to others?
3. How do the feelings from the previous two questions affect my urge to trust or share this information?

In the **Digital Detective's Evidence Locker**, under the tab for this chapter, you'll find a high-resolution version of the flowchart in Figure 1.2, which shows the alignment between CASEL's competencies and news/information literacy.

Additionally, in each of the unit plans that make up Chapters 8, 9, and 10, you'll find that we've emphasized specific core competencies as part of the work students engage in. But for now, let's take a closer look at each of the three broad categories individually and how they relate to information literacy.

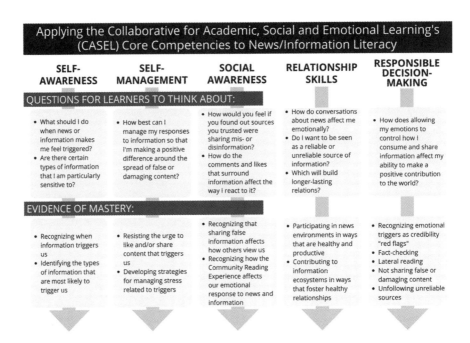

Figure 1.2 CASEL's five core competencies for social-emotional learning align closely with the foundational skills needed for applying the Trigger Lens.

Digital Detectives Think About How News Affects Them

Teaching kids to recognize language that is designed to trigger an emotion is an important part of applying the Triggers Lens. Many information literacy protocols ask learners to identify words or phrases that might be considered clickbait in the headline, but we have come to believe that this is insufficient and, largely, ineffective. Rather, we ask learners of all ages to first evaluate how the information they're being presented with makes them feel. By identifying and naming their emotional response, they can think logically about how to manage it (Torre & Lieberman, 2018). For younger kids, this might involve using an emotional Likert scale or mood meter, whereas older learners might accomplish the same goal by matching the emotion with corresponding physiological responses. (Check the **Digital Detective's Evidence Locker** for a mini-lesson that supports this work.) From there, we can challenge kids to look for patterns by identifying the specific words, phrases, images, or other media that trigger them. For example, while one learner may find information related to climate change and weather disasters to be particularly frightening, the learner sitting next to them may not share that response. Most importantly, however, the Triggers Lens is designed to help Digital Detectives recognize that these emotional responses are a signal to press pause.

Digital Detectives Press Pause

Rollo May described freedom as "the capacity to pause in the face of stimuli from many directions at once and, in this pause, to throw one's weight toward this response rather than that one" (1981). The fight-or-flight response in our brain robs us of that freedom, negatively influencing our ability to parse credibility and make good decisions. One of the goals of the Triggers Lens, therefore, is to arm Digital Detectives with the tools for retraining their brains to pause and think clearly. Digital Detectives must possess an understanding of what content may elicit an extreme emotion and also be ready to employ strategies for managing those emotions when they are triggered.

Basic mindfulness techniques—such as deep breathing, exercise, hydration, and processing emotion through conversation or journaling—can go a long way toward helping to manage the emotional stress that can render us incapable of making good news/information literacy decisions. In the **Digital Detective's Evidence Locker**, you'll find an infographic in which we walk Digital Detectives through the process of identifying and managing these emotional responses. However, we recommend providing learners with multiple opportunities, in a variety of contexts, to develop the habit of thinking about how their emotions affect their decisions. Several of the This Lens in Action mini-lessons at the end of this chapter were created to support this work.

As we noted in the Introduction, no single lens represents a "Stop: Go Directly to Jail" card. The presence of emotional triggers in a video, meme, article, or news broadcast alone does not mean the information is false. Instead, Digital Detectives should look at their presence as a credibility red flag—a signal that it's time to press pause and then, once the emotions have been managed, either dig deeper to determine credibility or abandon the information as being too risky to continue pursuing. For this reason, it's not enough for Digital Detectives to be able to recognize when information is triggering them. They must also be skilled at identifying why it may be triggering to others.

Digital Detectives Think About How News Affects Others

In Chapter 2, we'll take a deep dive into how the device and platform through which we access information profoundly affects our ability to determine its credibility, but for now, an important thing to keep in mind is that because so much of the information we consume is accessed through social media (Walker, 2019), this also means that much of it is being fed to us secondhand: We find it through someone in our network who, although sharing it, likely didn't create it. This matters because in that context, information is often packaged alongside the emotional response of the person sharing it.

For example, if your Uncle Larry reposts an article about a recent election on his Facebook timeline, as someone who is connected to Larry, chances are, you won't just be exposed to the emotional triggers in the post itself. In addition, you'll likely get some editorial from Larry, which, depending on your relationship, may trigger a variety of emotions.

Still, even if what triggers Uncle Larry to share his political opinions online aren't the same things that trigger you, Digital Detective work requires us to understand when language or other pieces of media are intended to trigger an emotional response, even when those plans don't work on us. What's more, while this step may certainly help learners spot additional credibility red flags, we think this step also offers us the opportunity to activate empathy as a tool to help learners connect the dots between their own behavior online and how it may affect others. Although we often challenge learners to consider how their relationship to a source affects their ability to determine its credibility, Digital Detectives must also understand how our collective reactions to information affect our ability to form and maintain long-lasting and healthy relationships with others, especially with those who may not share our beliefs.

Digital Detectives Make Responsible Decisions

When we talk to kids about their responsibility as digital citizens, those conversations often revolve around bullying and how anonymity online can influence unhealthy behavior. These conversations are important, but we think that news/information literacy offers us another opportunity to consider how our online behavior affects others and, by extension, affects our own credibility and reputation.

When applying the Triggers Lens with middle and high school learners, we can harness their developmental journey to activate empathy and more responsible online behavior. Tweens and teens care deeply about how others perceive them. And at that age, we have an opportunity to help them see their online behavior as a tool for shaping those identities. Many of today's young people aspire to be social media influencers (Saldanha, 2019), and indeed, some of them have already started the work of creating accounts and channels with thousands if not millions of followers. However, even if the kids you work with have other ambitions, many have begun to understand how reckless behavior posted online can damage their reputations, putting future college and/or job opportunities in jeopardy. The Triggers Lens can be used to help them see how sharing and spreading false information similarly affects how others perceive them and, ultimately, whether or not they trust them.

Younger kids can benefit from this work, too. Although they may not be ready to think about their online reputations just yet, even the youngest Digital Detectives can make connections between how information makes them feel and the fact that by sharing information that makes them feel bad, they are taking actions to make others feel bad, too. When a group of kindergarteners enters a school library for the first time (and perhaps even the second, third, or twentieth time), they often have to be shown how to respect boundaries and to use their voices and bodies in ways that make them a good friend, listener, and learner. While we'll talk more about how the lenses apply to K–3 learners in Chapter 5, Digital Detectives in Grades 4–12 can apply those same **dispositions** to information literacy. Although the characteristics that make them a good friend, listener, and learner while sitting crisscross-applesauce might be a little different, the desire to exhibit behavior that makes them responsible and trustworthy within their community is a branch from the same tree.

Putting First Things First

In 2018, researcher Susan Currie Sivek wrote: "news literacy education has long focused on the significance of facts, sourcing, and verifiability. While these are critical aspects of news, rapidly developing emotion analytics technologies intended to respond to and even alter digital news audiences' emotions also demand that we pay greater attention to the role of emotion in news consumption." For educators, this represents an opportunity. In many ways, news literacy and SEL efforts have a lot in common. Both require learners to develop new ways of thinking. Both benefit from partnerships between school personnel and families. Both are most likely to be successful when integrated across content areas. And both seek to help kids develop healthy behaviors that will serve them both in and out of school.

We created the Triggers Lens as the first step in our protocol for growing Digital Detectives because we recognize that without this first step, the others are moot. However, as you'll notice in the next few chapters, all of the other lenses are influenced by this one. There's not a single aspect of information literacy that isn't tied, in some way, to our emotional response to the information we consume. In *Team Human*, Douglas Rushkoff wrote,

> Any of our healthy social mechanisms can become vulnerabilities— what hackers would call "exploits" for those who want to manipulate us. When a charity encloses a free "gift" of return address labels along with its solicitation for a donation, it is consciously manipulating our ancient, embedded social bias for reciprocity. The example is trivial, but the pattern is universal. We either succumb to the pressure with the inner knowledge that something is off, or we recognize the ploy, reject the plea, and arm ourselves against such tactics in the future. (2019)

Terms of Detection

Emotional Triggers: Content that triggers an extreme emotional response. That response often makes us feel uncomfortable, but it can also elicit feelings of euphoria or superiority. The key to a trigger is that when pulled, emotion takes over and drives our decision-making. Once triggered, we have to work harder to engage the logical parts of our brain.

Fight-or-Flight Response: The instinctive physiological response to a threatening situation, which readies us to either resist with force or flee the situation.

Firewall: A physical or ideological barrier designed to protect against the spread of danger; sometimes applied to the ideological separation that prevented journalists from being influenced by advertisers or other revenue streams.

Disposition: A person's inherent qualities or habits.

Credit: Finish This Comic!
by Jarrett Lerner

This Lens in Action:
Mini-Lessons to Try Tomorrow

Check the section tab marked Chapter 1 in the **Digital Detective's Evidence Locker** for a number of mini-lessons (ML) to help Digital Detectives sharpen their skills related to the Triggers Lens. Some examples include:

- An Information Literacy Likert Scale/Mood Meter
- Speed or Brake Activity
- Finish This Comic! Activity by Jarrett Lerner
- Plus more!

In some ways, this tie to our instinctive emotional responses makes Digital Detective work daunting, because by beginning with Triggers, we are acknowledging that we are a part of the problem. If our emotions are what's causing us (at least in part) to trust and spread false information, then we have only ourselves to blame when those choices come back to haunt us. But in another, more significant way, we find the Triggers Lens profoundly empowering, because if the problems are within us, so too are the solutions.

The Second Lens: Access

Reminder: A variety of resources related to this chapter can be found in the **Digital Detective's Evidence Locker**. Use the QR code to the left, or visit evidencelocker.online, then navigate to Chapter 2.

> When reading online news, the closest source is often one of our friends. Because we tend to trust our friends, our cognitive filters weaken, making a social media feed fertile ground for fake news to sneak into our consciousness.... The persuasive appeal of peers over experts is compounded by the fact that we tend to let our guard down even more when we encounter news in our personal space.
>
> —S. Shyam Sundar

Explore This Lens

When writing *Fact vs. Fiction: Teaching Critical Thinking Skills in the Age of Fake News*, we spent a lot of time thinking about how smartphones should turn existing news and media literacy efforts on their ears. Spoiler alert: That hasn't happened (yet). In 2018, when that book was published, roughly 83% of the information Americans consumed was accessed through a mobile device (Anderson & Jiang, 2018). Unsurprisingly, in the years that have followed, that number has continued to rise. As of 2020, 5.24 billion people (roughly 67% of the total population) owned a mobile phone (GSMA, 2020). To put that in perspective, according to the World

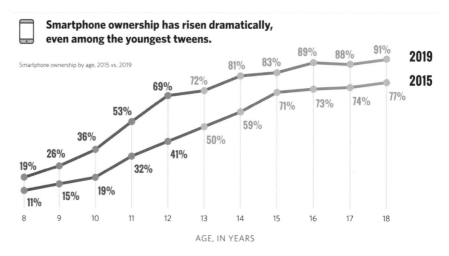

Smartphone ownership has risen dramatically, even among the youngest tweens.

Smartphone ownership by age, 2015 vs. 2019

2019
2015

AGE, IN YEARS

Figure 2.1 Common Sense Media's 2019 Common Sense Census showed an increase in smartphone usage for all ages.

Health Organization, only 3.8 billion people have access to running water in their homes or dwellings (WHO & UNICEF, 2020). While these disparities are shocking, they are also very telling. How does this translate to kids? We're glad you asked!

Every four years, Common Sense Media conducts a large-scale study exploring how U.S. kids age 8 to 18 use media throughout their daily lives, both at school and home. The 2019 Common Sense Census exposed some eye-opening truths. For example, by age 11, 53% of young people own or have access to a smartphone (Figure 2.1). By the time they enter high school, these numbers are much, much higher (Rideout & Robb, 2019).

These findings should be profoundly informed by data collected from the Pew Research Center in the same year, which found that news consumers overwhelmingly turn to their mobile devices, rather than to a laptop or desktop, to find out what's happening in the world (Walker, 2019). And yet, when we visit schools around the country to help educators develop media literacy lessons, we find the exact opposite to be true. In school, the vast majority of news literacy instruction still occurs with the devices that our kids are least likely to use when information isn't being consumed for an assignment. This matters for a variety of reasons. Here are just a few:

- From the same source, the same news story looks *vastly different* when viewed on a mobile device versus a traditional browser.

- The same news story varies greatly in appearance when viewed on two *different apps*. For example, while news stories on Instagram often require users to search the account's bio for links to additional information, the same story in TikTok might require users to view several consecutive videos for more information, or search in the comments for video replies.

- The ways in which students locate the information that is commonly required to determine credibility (author, date of publication, the editorial stance of the publication, etc.) also varies widely depending on the app they use to view the story.

In short, the strategies being taught in school to help young people differentiate fact from fiction in the information they consume often do not transfer to the ways in which they access, react to, and share information in every other location (when, frankly, the stakes are much higher). As Paul Barnwell explained in the article "Do Smartphones Have a Place in the Classroom?" (2016), "If educators do not find ways to leverage mobile technology in all learning environments, for all students, then we are failing our kids by not adequately preparing them to make the connection between their world outside of school and their world inside school."

Access and Equity

Centering mobile devices in our news and information literacy instruction is also a moral imperative. Kids in low-income families are more dependent on mobile devices (and public Wi-Fi) when completing homework assignments. In addition to being easily personalized, these devices are supremely portable, which is important when only 45% of low-income families have access to broadband internet at home (Walker, 2019). Smartphones are easier to transport than a laptop to the neighborhood library, coffee shop, or fast food restaurant where Wi-Fi is readily available. Additionally, while laptops are becoming more and more economical, a mobile phone can also replace

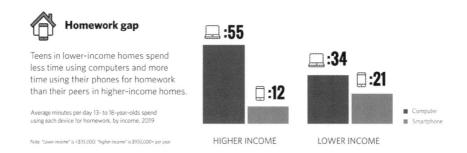

Homework gap

Teens in lower-income homes spend less time using computers and more time using their phones for homework than their peers in higher-income homes.

Average minutes per day 13- to 18-year-olds spend using each device for homework, by income, 2019

Note: "Lower income" is <$35,000; "higher income" is $100,000+ per year

💻 :55   💻 :34   📱 :21   📱 :12

■ Computer
■ Smartphone

HIGHER INCOME   LOWER INCOME

Figure 2.2 Common Sense Media's 2019 Common Sense Census showed that lower-income families rely heavily on smartphones for homework.

the need for a landline. Only providing learners with skills for determining information credibility while using a laptop or desktop creates an opportunity gap that leaves our poorest students behind. The penetration of mobile devices among all households makes using them as the primary tool to teach information literacy a no-brainer. Because these are the devices that our most vulnerable families are most likely to rely on when tackling school work (Figure 2.2), they must take center stage in our teaching practice.

Figure 2.3 Banning mobile phones in school prevents Digital Detectives from learning how to parse credibility on the devices they interact with most.

No Phone Zones

That said, we understand that for a variety of reasons, some schools have policies prohibiting students from accessing their mobile devices during class time (Figure 2.3). There are a number of ways for you to work around these restrictions while preparing students to be Digital Detectives.

- **Use your phone!** Place your device under a document camera, and then once students have walked through the steps of the credibility protocol for a story on the web, do it together using your phone. You can ask students to tell you where to tap while you model the procedure.

- **Use donated devices.** Lots of families have old phones lying in drawers collecting dust. It would only take a handful of these, connected to your school's guest Wi-Fi, to enable learners to work in small groups to accomplish the same task.

- 🔎 **Go analog.** Screenshots of news stories taken from mobile devices enable students to at least think about the places on the phone they might tap if they were using a real device. (See Figure 2.5 in the "Digital Detectives Peel Back the Layers" section for an example.)

- 🔎 **Talk to your admin.** Use this learning as an opportunity to chat with administrators about getting permission to lift the smartphone ban, in the library only, for lessons on media/news literacy. If you come armed with information and passion for making a difference for kids, you might just find the flexibility you need.

The Community Reading Experience

None of our students are old enough to remember the beginnings of the internet. The earliest iterations of the World Wide Web were intended only to link resources across computers. The purpose was to preserve and make truth more accessible. With the benefit of hindsight, we can see now that as the internet grew, it actually created "an impenetrable thicket of pointers, from one resource to another to another to another until it becomes nearly impossible to discern an ultimate source of truth" (Pesce, 2020).

In *Fact vs. Fiction*, we explored the idea of filter bubbles and how our own search habits and the ability to personalize our online experiences have led to filtered experiences in which our beliefs are consistently confirmed. This personalization is most prevalent in mobile devices in which the entire experience is designed to increase engagement (Figure 2.4). As with every aspect of our digital lives, this too has had unintended consequences. As the saying goes, "First we shape our tools, thereafter our tools shape us" (Pesce, 2020).

In addition to how mobile devices add layers to the steps Digital Detectives must take when analyzing clues about a source's credibility, so too do they complicate the ways in which information can trigger extreme emotional responses. In Chapter 1, we explored the idea that emotional triggers spark reactions that may cause us to act in careless or even harmful ways: trusting

Figure 2.4 It's no accident that the features used for engaging with content are placed in what's known as the "thumb zone," the area easiest to reach with our thumb while holding our device with one hand.

and sharing information without fully vetting it. With that in mind, if emotional triggers act as the spark, then the **Community Reading Experience** that defines how content is consumed on mobile devices is surely the kindling. It's up to Digital Detectives to recognize this combustible combination before a firestorm of misinformation becomes too difficult to control.

Engagement metrics are formulas that measure the number of interactions that content shared on social media generates. Examples include likes (or other reactions), comments, and shares. The more engagement a post garners, the more frequently it appears on our feeds. We've come to think of the term "influencer" as referring to the ability of popular content creators to influence their audience, but this term has as much to do with the ways that our engagement with their content influences the algorithms that drive our feeds (Sehl, 2019).

Engagement metrics affect us in other ways, too. In *Fact vs. Fiction*, we created a "Fake News Self-Assessment" in which educators were challenged to determine whether stories presented on mobile devices were real or fabricated. In the years since that book was published, we've had the opportunity to use that survey with hundreds, even thousands, of educators (and often their students), which revealed some interesting trends. Chief among them is the fact that like/share counts shape our perception of what can be trusted. When we asked both adult and school-aged learners to think deeply about what aspects of a specific story fooled them in the self-assessment, one consistent response was how other people reacted to the same information. In short, the more likes, comments, and shares a post or video receives, the more trustworthy it becomes in the eyes of consumers.

On the other hand, low engagement counts or significant "thumbs down" reactions from the community can inspire distrust of content or of those sharing it. As a result, in recent years we've seen an increase in coordinated efforts to weaponize features of the Community Reading Experience in order to inflict harm. In 2016, Reddit users organized a "one-star blitz" of Megyn Kelly's then-new book, *Settle for More*. The plan was simple: tens of thousands of Redditors would leave anonymous, scathing, one-star reviews for the book on the websites of major booksellers. The goal was threefold: bring down the average rating, flood the feeds that surround the product with negativity, and, most importantly, destroy book sales and Kelly's reputation. It worked. By weaponizing the Community Reading Experience, Kelly's critics were able to sabotage her book launch (Waldman, 2016). In the internet age, this hive-like behavior is sometimes referred to as **cancel culture**. Although sometimes lobbed as a political football to discredit legitimate consequences for harmful behavior, for the purposes of this book, we are using the term to refer to the trend of weaponizing social media to ruin an individual or organization's reputation. Often this takes the form of simply flooding social media with negative content relating to the person or group. However, cancel culture can also take on more dangerous forms, such as doxxing: posting someone's personal information (address or license plate number, for example) online in order to facilitate face-to-face conflicts or cause personal or professional harm.

In response to the Megyn Kelly incident, Amazon (and other platforms) took steps to weaken the effect of reviews left by people who hadn't actually purchased the product from their site by labeling reviews linked to purchases as being "verified." Social media platforms soon followed suit by prioritizing comments left by those we follow. These steps may have been marketed as ways to help combat the trend of using site features as weapons, but they also served as yet another strategy for increasing engagement with content. Including information about other people in our networks who have endorsed content by liking or sharing it makes us want to do the same. For example, in addition to seeing the total number of likes a post on Instagram receives, users now see the names of their friends who liked that post, too.

In her book *Who Do We Choose To Be?: Facing Reality, Claiming Leadership, Restoring Sanity*, Margaret Wheatly wrote, "One reason identities slam shut is that other greater human needs supersede openness, curiosity, and intelligence. We need to belong. We need to feel accepted" (2017, p. 180). We often think of peer pressure as being bullied into doing something in an aggressive way, but the urge to belong is far stronger and subtler. When we see the name of someone we know next to a tiny heart emoji on social media, by tapping that same heart, we're drawing attention to the fact that we share something in common with that person (and many others)—even if that something is just a tendency to endorse information without fully vetting it.

Teach This Lens: Access

This is why the second lens through which Digital Detectives must examine information is the Access Lens. This lens requires Digital Detectives to consider how the device through which they consume information affects their ability to determine its credibility. Before trusting, sharing, or otherwise endorsing information they find online, Digital Detectives must first ask themselves a series of questions related to the device they are using:

1. How does the device (and/or app) affect my ability to locate traditional markers of credibility (such as author, date of publication, etc.)?
2. How does the Community Reading Experience affect my urge to trust or share this information?
3. Is the way I'm using my device affecting how I interact with or respond to information?

Answers to these questions can be credibility red flags, and Digital Detectives must learn to look at them as clues. (Check the **Digital Detective's Evidence Locker** for an infographic to help students understand the questions that define the Access Lens.)

Digital Detectives Peel Back the Layers

In Chapter 3, we'll take a deeper dive into the specifics of how the Digital Detective work of searching for credibility clues continues to evolve, but for now one thing remains essential: whatever credibility markers we ask our learners to search for, we must teach them how to locate and evaluate them on mobile devices.

At the beginning of 2020, when it seemed as though the Australian wildfires would likely be the biggest story of the year (clearly, we were wrong!), we captured two screenshots of the same story, published by the same source, in order to illustrate how different they looked when accessed on two different devices (Figure 2.5).

Mobile devices create an environment that requires students to dig a bit deeper to locate basic information common in many credibility protocols. For example, when looking at the story posted on Instagram, finding answers to the following questions is tougher:

Accessed from mobile device. App: Instagram

Accessed from New York Times website using Chrome browser on a laptop.

Figure 2.5 The same news story can look vastly different depending on where it's viewed.

- What date was this story published? Is that different from the date it was posted?
- Who is the author? Is that different from who shared it on social media?
- How do we locate information about the source itself?

It is also important to note that the answers to these questions may be quite different when viewing the same story on a different app.

By contrast, websites tend to provide more information about the source without our having to click further. For example:

- The article contains a headline that can be evaluated for click-bait and emotional triggers.
- The publication date and information about when the story was last updated is on the front page.
- The website URL gives us clues about the original source.

We can't possibly know all the steps for locating credibility clues in every app on every device. However, we can and must give our learners the opportunity to build those bridges of understanding themselves. Only by allowing them to compare and contrast those steps as part of their information literacy work are we truly preparing them to be Digital Detectives. (Check the **Digital Detective's Evidence Locker** for a mini-lesson to help facilitate the work of comparing and contrasting these elements.)

As we noted earlier in the chapter, the interactive features that surround information when accessed in apps on a mobile device make it easy for us to lean into the extreme emotional responses that information often elicits. All those features (such as like and share counts) that frame every photo, video, and story that we see may seem superfluous, but they are actually incredibly potent. Digital Detectives must understand how the Community Reading Experience contributes to how information triggers emotions that affect our decisions.

Digital Detectives Think About How News Affects Them

The ease with which we can like, share, or comment on a photo, post, or video is one of the features that make social media so popular. It often takes as little as a single tap or swipe for us to show our like (or dislike) for the content we consume. Challenging learners to think deeply about how these and other elements of the Community Reading Experience affect their urge to trust or share information is the first step in helping them avoid missteps. Thinking metacognitively about how these features influence them takes practice, but in our experience the juice, as they say, is worth the squeeze. (Check the **Digital Detective's Evidence Locker** for a mini-lesson that supports this work.)

Digital Detectives Think About How News Affects Others

Digital Detective work requires that once learners understand how features of the Community Reading Experience affect them as individuals, they must then also consider how the same elements of a story or post may, in turn, spark similar reactions in others. In addition to like and share counts, comments (and their associated engagement metrics) are an important part of this equation.

While many apps now show us which members of our friend group also reacted to or shared a post, even more now prioritize comments defaulting to what are often referred to as "top comments." Top comments may include those by people you know or are connected to, but they are more often prioritized based on the number of engagements the user or their specific comment has generated. For example, if a comment made three days ago has received more reactions (positive or negative) than one added three minutes ago, the older comment will appear at the top of our comments feed. Of course, this also is true with apps that feature lists of subjects that are currently "trending" or receiving the most interactions. The idea that what's trending is based on engagement is nothing new. However, it's important to remember that as we noted in Chapter 1, negative and salacious content tends to garner more engagement online than positive or even neutral content. In short, it's often the scream that rises to the top when it comes to social media.

With this in mind, Digital Detectives must be armed with the understanding that "top comments" are not necessarily (and in fact are unlikely to be) the most accurate or helpful in understanding the original content. But more than that, it's helpful for learners to consider what about that content may have triggered the types of responses that generate the most engagement. If those top comments feel fraught with emotion, what about the original content pushed those buttons? Understanding why someone may have reacted in an extreme way to specific information can help Digital Detectives avoid the trap of allowing those comments to become triggers in and of themselves. But even more importantly, that understanding can build empathy within the community. (Check the **Digital Detective's Evidence Locker** for a mini-lesson that supports this work.)

Digital Detectives Make Responsible Decisions

With so many of today's learners keen on becoming social media influencers themselves, understanding how the Community Reading Experience affects the urge to trust and share provides a bridge between content consumer and creator roles. As Digital Detectives become more aware of the nuances that exist between information that was designed to inform and information that was created to influence, they can then apply that knowledge to the content they create and share themselves. Engaging learners in the task or considering how the decisions they make as a content creator affect their own engagement can be a powerful tool in helping them recognize those same decisions when made by others. (Check the **Digital Detective's Evidence Locker** for a mini-lesson that supports this work.)

Digital Detectives Take Control of Their Devices

In *Fact vs. Fiction*, we shared some strategies for helping learners disrupt the algorithms that influence the content we see online. A few of those tips include:

- Use your device's settings to limit which apps are able to send you notifications.
- Clear the browser history on your phone to disrupt filter bubbles.
- Use "reader view" in your browser app to avoid sponsored ads.

In addition, you can offer Digital Detectives these tips to help them take control of their devices, instead of letting those devices take control of them:

- Search for setting defaults in apps that prioritize some comments over others. Many apps will allow you to change those settings so that comments appear in chronological order.

- Mute conversations when they get too loud. Many apps allow you to mute a specific post or even a user. Muting content simply means that you won't see it any longer without having to unfriend or disconnect from a specific user. Depending on the app, these settings can be either temporary or permanent. Because the engagement around a post drives how frequently it appears in our feeds, muting content is a useful tool for disrupting this system.

It's Elementary, My Dear Watson

In the same way that you'll find that the Triggers Lens is embedded in all subsequent lenses, it's impossible to divorce the role of mobile devices from any other aspect of Digital Detective work. In Chapter 3, we'll unpack new thinking about how to search for credibility clues when fact-checking content, but even the most innovative approach is rendered ineffective when we fail to build bridges between how these strategies play out on a desktop or laptop versus the way they unfold on the mobile devices that are present in so much of our lives. Just as today's police detectives no longer use the kinds of tools famed fictional detective Sherlock Holmes relied on, so too must Digital Detectives be armed with strategies that are commensurate with the era in which they live. While few classrooms or libraries are flush with the latest and greatest technology, if we hope to help our learners grow into the kinds of Digital Detectives that our world needs, we must find ways to include the devices that they use most.

Terms of Detection

Community Reading Experience: The social experience of consuming content online, especially through mobile devices. The features that contribute to this experience include likes, shares, and comments, along with the public counts associated with each element.

Engagement Metrics: The number of interaction elements the Community Reading Experience generates. For example, the more likes or shares a post or video receives, the higher its engagement metrics.

Cancel Culture: The trend of weaponizing social media to ruin the reputation of an individual or organization. The targets of these attacks are referred to as being "cancelled."

Mobile VS Traditional

Comparing/contrasting the steps in detecting credibility clues on a mobile device vs a laptop or desktop.

SOURCE	CREDIBILITY MARKERS	WEB	MOBILE	REFLECTION

Mobile vs. Traditional: Compare and Contrast Activity

This Lens in Action:
Mini-Lessons to Try Tomorrow

Check the section tab marked Chapter 2 in the **Digital Detective's Evidence Locker** for a number of mini-lessons (ML) to help Digital Detectives sharpen their skills related to the Access Lens. Some examples include:

- Mobile vs. Traditional: Compare and Contrast Activities
- Community Reading Experience: Seek and Find Activity
- Finish This Comic! Activity by Jarrett Lerner
- Plus more!

The Third Lens: Forensics

Reminder: A variety of resources related to this chapter can be found in the **Digital Detective's Evidence Locker**. Use the QR code to the left, or visit evidencelocker.online, then navigate to Chapter 3.

> Facts are stubborn things; and whatever may be our wishes, our inclinations, or the dictates of our passions, they cannot alter the state of facts and evidence.
>
> —U.S. President John Adams

Explore This Lens

In criminology, the word *forensics* refers to detectives' techniques to locate, collect, and process evidence found during an investigation. When detectives are called to a scene, their first job is to look for evidence to determine whether a crime has been committed. If it appears one has, then evidence collection, processing, and evaluation continues until the facts of the case lead to a suspect. It is the forensic evidence that sometimes offers insight into the motives of the person behind the illegal activity. And sometimes, clues from one case inform detective work in previously unrelated cases. Each clue is a puzzle piece that, alone, fails to answer central questions about the mystery. Taken together, however, those pieces form a more complete picture.

For Digital Detectives, the word **forensics** means much the same thing, referring to the process of locating, collecting, and evaluating *digital clues* that provide insight into the credibility of the information. Just as criminal detectives follow the clues to form theories, their digital counterparts must seek evidence to help them crack the case. Instructional strategies and tools for this work have been around for nearly as long as the internet itself, and we're guessing that you are familiar with quite a few, which we'll unpack later in the chapter. The most popular of these protocols were created primarily by educators whose concerns about false information mirror our own. As our digital lives evolve and the ways we engage with information become more fluid, personalized, and designed with neuroscience in mind, the less relevant and effective these checklist and mnemonic devices are—and yet, they persist.

Oh, CRAAP

If you have a poster with some version of the CRAAP Test hanging in your classroom or library, you are not alone. If you've asked your students to use the CARS Checklist, the RADCAB protocol, the SMELL test, the SIFT Method, or some other checklist to determine whether information can be trusted, you are in good company. These tools for determining information credibility remain remarkably popular in large part because they are so easy to implement. After all, what middle schooler *isn't* going to remember a mnemonic device that sounds a lot like a bodily function? (Turns out, quite a few. But we'll get to that later.) Plus, for busy teachers, the promise of a silver bullet, a one-and-done strategy for determining fact from fiction, is appealing. In reality, however, true fact-checking is messy, time-consuming, and expensive. As editors from ProPublica noted in 2017, the public doesn't always understand the depth and expense of true fact-checking, which doesn't relieve journalists from this work, but gives the false impression that it should be easy (Kiernan). In *Fact vs. Fiction*, we wondered, if credibility resources and checklists like the CRAAP Test are so great, why aren't they working in the 21st century? Since that book came out, we think we know (at least part of) the answer.

Many of these tools have been around for a long time. The CRAAP Test, for example, was created in 2004, three years before the first iPhone was released, one year before YouTube hosted its first video, two years before Facebook would be available to anyone other than college students, two years before Twitter, six years before Instagram, and 12 years before TikTok (McFadden, 2020). Sarah Blakeslee, who created the CRAAP Test while working as a librarian for California State University, Chico, could never have imagined how the information landscape would change over time and to what degree those changes would render her method of looking for credibility clues inadequate. But that's exactly what has happened. The world has changed a great deal since 2004, and nowhere is that more evident than in our digital spaces. Unfortunately, instructional strategies for navigating the digital world safely and effectively haven't kept pace.

The Shift from Identifying to Investigating

In 2017, researchers at the Stanford History Education Group (SHEG) published a paper titled "Lateral Reading: Reading Less and Learning More When Evaluating Digital Information." In it, they posited that one of the primary reasons that checklists like the CRAAP Test don't work is because they require learners to look only within the website itself for clues (Wineberg & McGrew, 2017). While the letters making up the different mnemonics vary, all these checklists require learners to locate and label some version of the same credibility markers: the source/author, the date of publication, examples of false claims, and evidence of bias. Students using a checklist like this are tasked with scrolling down the page, searching for examples (or non-examples), so they can check off each box. This is known as *vertical reading* because the process requires learners only to scroll up and down. More importantly, however, tasking students to simply scan a page for information matching items in a checklist requires little more brain power than the average word search.

Researchers at SHEG encourage learners to approach information literacy like a fact-checker (Wineberg & McGrew, 2017). Michael Caulfield, Director of Blended and Networked Learning at Washington State University

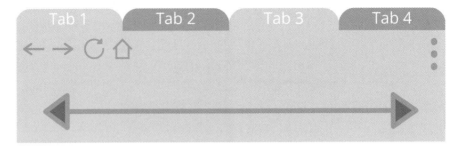

Figure 3.1 To read laterally, fact-checkers open new tabs in order to search for more information.

Vancouver, put it this way: "Fact-checkers [understand] that 'the web' is not a metaphor: To learn about a single node you must see where it fits in a larger network" (as quoted in Kamenetz, 2017). That's not to say that the clues that traditional news/information protocols (like CRAAP) ask learners to look for are irrelevant. However, instead of relying on the unlikely possibility that creators of false information are going to leave clues to their misdeeds within the content itself, we have to assume that they've done their best to *hide* such evidence. Just as police detectives must take their initial investigations beyond the crime scene itself to verify or understand the clues found in the original location, so too must Digital Detectives expand the scope of their investigations to include other sources. Clues found within the original source are starting points only: red flags that raise questions and build new curiosities we can answer only by extending our search.

Researchers at SHEG refer to this work as **lateral reading** because it requires learners to open new tabs in their browsers to seek additional information about the content, its source, and their potential motivations (Wineberg & McGrew, 2017). Rather than reading vertically, fact-checkers read across or laterally (Figure 3.1).

We think lateral reading is an important next step in the evolution of digital detective work. But we don't think it goes quite far enough.

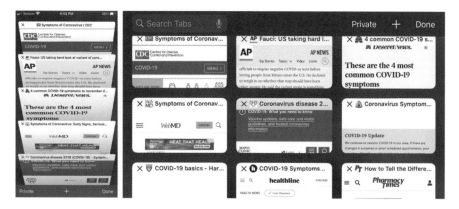

Figure 3.2 On a mobile device nothing about the investigative process looks "lateral."

Neither Vertical nor Lateral

We believe traditional information literacy protocols fail because even if kids were motivated to complete a checklist, or read laterally every time they come into contact with new information, those strategies often don't make sense when applied to the devices kids use most. Chapter 2 examined how mobile devices have redefined how we engage with and are affected by information, with even our youngest learners accessing and using mobile devices with increasing regularity. Indeed, more than one-third of parents with a child under 12 say their child began interacting with a smartphone before the age of 5. Nearly one in five parents of a child younger than 12 say their child has their own smartphone (Grieco, 2020). However, our instructional strategies for preparing learners for today's world continue to be rooted in the technology of the past. Even a strategy as important as lateral reading assumes that students will be searching for information on a desktop or laptop browser. The two screenshots in Figure 3.2 capture the way multiple tabs, related to a single search (in this case, for information on the COVID-19 virus), look on a mobile device: in no way do they appear to be organized laterally.

But wait . . . we're assuming that this search originated within a browser app on the device. What if this investigation was originally inspired by a TikTok video or Instagram post? Chances are, if Digital Detectives were curious about the credibility of the information in that post, they'd first take a look at the user's profile or perhaps take stock of information in the comments or other aspects of the Community Reading Experience. From there, they may be led down a rabbit hole of other links, perhaps finally finding their way to a browser to do more targeted searching. This complex, multistep process requires Digital Detectives to bounce among the links, apps, and sources, discovering patterns in the noise. Caulfield referred to this as "teleportation" and posited that traditional analog reading sits within an established context: "When you start to read a book, journal article or a physical newspaper in the 'real world,' you already know a bit about your source" (as quoted in Kamenetz, 2017). Whereas, he continued, in online reading that context is constantly changing and teleporting readers from one context to the next, each of which has a bearing on credibility. While lateral reading accounts for the idea of moving between sources, that movement is often not linear.

The Multidirectional Nature of Authentic Investigations

For fans of true crime or detective stories in pop culture, the investigative process is virtually synonymous with large bulletin boards or walls covered in a case's evidence with important connections linked by bits of yarn, string, or lines drawn with markers. These tools are known by a number of names, but one that stands out to us is the *link board*. Like those included at the start of every "Teach This Lens" section, link boards visually capture the true complexity of digital investigations. Using the credibility red flags present in the initial source as a jumping-off point, today's Digital Detectives must then expand their searches to include other apps, platforms, widgets, browser extensions, and tabs.

However, even more significant is this: The path these investigations take must be inspired by authentic inquiry and not by whatever letter comes next in a checklist. Rather than follow any single direction, Digital Detectives must be empowered to take their investigations wherever the clues lead them. For Digital Detectives, forensics work requires more than a checklist or mnemonic device, no matter how clever it may be. We believe multidirectional investigations combined with meaningful questions inspired by the evidence are vital in helping build bridges between the research that kids do in school for an assignment and the kind they do at home, when the consequences for falling for false information may be far more significant.

Teach This Lens: Forensics

This is why the third lens through which Digital Detectives must examine information is the Forensics Lens. Only after managing their emotional response to information and considering how the device they are using may affect their ability to parse credibility are Digital Detectives ready to investigate the evidence and follow it to the facts of the case. Just as Maslow reminds us that only after learners' basic needs are met are they truly able to concentrate on the work of learning (1943), so too must Digital Detectives manage their cognitive responses to information before they can parse its credibility. We believe the following questions are central to this work:

1. What credibility red flags have I already identified in the information itself?

2. What are the most important questions that these red flags raise and/or that I *must* be able to answer in order to determine whether this information can be trusted?

3. What effect does the format of the information have on the path of my investigation?

Answers to these questions are clues that should inform a Digital Detective's investigation. (Check the **Digital Detective's Evidence Locker** for an infographic to help students understand the questions that define the Forensics Lens.)

Digital Detectives Ask the Right Questions

In many ways, the first two lenses are tools to help Digital Detectives form effective questions to be explored during the investigative process essential to the Forensic Lens. For example, in addition to assisting learners to navigate their own emotional response to information, the Triggers Lens also challenges them to take stock of how emotions affect our urge to trust and share content without fully vetting it *and* how some content creators count on those responses. Once those emotions are identified, the Forensics Lens challenges learners to ask questions for further investigation, such as "Who benefits if I share this information without evaluating it?" or "Does this emotional response align with the biases or agenda of a specific person or group?" These questions can then guide the investigation, potentially leading Digital Detectives to more closely examine the motivations of the people who create information and/or the networks they rely on to amplify it. While the presence of emotional triggers alone is not enough to dismiss information as false, the red flags revealed by the Triggers Lens should help Digital Detectives form the questions that will lead them to more definitive evidence. For younger learners, simply practicing the skill of asking meaningful questions is an important part of connecting the Triggers and Forensics Lenses. From there they can begin thinking about how specific emotional reactions link to certain types of questions. (Check the **Digital Detective's Evidence Locker** for mini-lessons to help Digital Detectives sharpen their skills for developing evidence-based questions.)

This is true for the Access Lens as well. Thinking about how a device changes the way we consume and interact with information may also inform the questions Digital Detectives ask as part of the investigative process necessary to the Forensic Lens. For example, the Access Lens pushes students to consider the layers that a mobile device may add to the process of identifying basic information about the content they are consuming. With this in mind, some questions to further guide the investigation might be: "What are the app-specific steps I need to take in order to determine if the person/account sharing this information is also responsible for creating it?" or "How can I tell if this is a verified account? Does this app identify when the account has been verified?" Taken alone, the answers to these questions may not be enough to determine whether content should be trusted or dismissed, but in combination with the answers to other questions, they can help Digital Detectives form a more complete credibility picture.

Digital Detectives Must Be Transliterate

One of the reasons digital content is so notoriously difficult to evaluate lies in its inability to be just one thing. We tend to think of Instagram as a tool for exploring photos; the reality is that Instagram timelines are cluttered with text, video, advertisements, infographics, charts, graphs, headlines, hashtags, emojis, and, yes, photos. The same is true for an article published on any major journalistic outlet's website, an instructional video hosted on YouTube, a politician's tweet, or a recipe shared by your aunt on Facebook. Although we may think of an article or post as *one* piece of information, these singular artifacts are likely made up of multiple types of media. With that in mind, parsing credibility in today's world requires Digital Detectives to be **transliterate**, or able to apply critical analysis across media (Sukovic, 2016).

Of course, this is easier said than done, in large part because media formats are constantly evolving and changing shape. With ever-growing warnings about how emerging technology is being used to manipulate and harm us (O'Sullivan, 2019), it's tempting to seek out bulleted lists of tips for spotting suspect uses of the latest technology. If information literacy were a game of poker, a list of "tells" revealing weakness in those who create deep fakes or immersive data visualizations (for example) would be very handy indeed. But as with most card games, the house has the advantage when it comes to information literacy. Long before the digital ink has dried on the last bullet in our list, content creators have already improved their craft to levels that make our suggestions obsolete.

Instead, we must teach Digital Detectives to look at unique media formats as opportunities to apply each lens. Rather than thinking of a single article, post, or video as one thing to be evaluated, Digital Detectives must be trained to dissect artifacts into their individual parts, learning to identify those pieces that can be dismissed from the investigation and then applying each lens to those that remain. By looking at embedded media through the Triggers Lens, for example, Digital Detectives have the chance to think about how certain formats (such as videos or diagrams) affect their urge to trust or share information. These discoveries are springboards for deeper questions about the specific elements of some particularly effective/influential formats and how content creators might leverage them to further an agenda or influence engagement. From there, questions about who created the media being shared or what data was used to compile it become important points in the investigation.

More Questions, Less CRAAP

While we keep using the CRAAP Test as an example, the message we really want to send is that checklists alone do not constitute an information literacy strategy or plan. In addition to requiring very little critical thinking, they represent a binary that simply does not apply to how information is created, shared, and engaged with in the 21st century. There's no checklist in the world that will apply accurately to most, nevermind *all*, the content our young people come in contact with. Furthermore, just as the investigative process is neither wholly vertical nor lateral, so too is the answer to the question "Can this be trusted?" rarely a simple yes or no. For this reason, the Forensics Lens is far less about finding the right answer and much more about asking the right questions.

Terms of Detection

Forensics: The process of locating, collecting, and evaluating *digital clues* that provide insight into the credibility of the information.

Lateral Reading: The process of opening new tabs to search for more information about a source or topic in order to determine information credibility.

Transliteracy: A Digital Detective's ability to apply critical analysis across media.

Credit: Finish This Comic! by Jarrett Lerner

This Lens in Action:
Mini-Lessons to Try Tomorrow

Check the section tab marked Chapter 3 in the **Digital Detective's Evidence Locker** for a number of mini-lessons (ML) to help Digital Detectives sharpen their skills related to the Forensics Lens. Some examples include:

- Create Your Own Investigative Link Board
- What Makes a Good Question Activity
- Finish This Comic! Activity by Jarrett Lerner
- Plus more!

The Fourth Lens: Motives

Reminder: A variety of resources related to this chapter can be found in the **Digital Detective's Evidence Locker**. Use the QR code to the left or visit evidencelocker.online, then navigate to Chapter 4.

> Every time you open your phone or your computer, your brain is walking onto a battleground. The aggressors are the architects of your digital world, and their weapons are the apps, news feeds, and notifications in your field of view every time you look at a screen. They are all attempting to capture your most scarce resource—our attention—and take it hostage for money. Your captive attention is worth billions to them in advertising and subscription revenue.
>
> —Tobias Rose-Stockwell

Explore This Lens

In *Fact vs. Fiction*, we shared the story of Dimitri, a teenager in Macedonia who was making a small fortune (compared to others in his home country) creating false news stories targeting American voters. Dimitri's example is upsetting in part because he is so flippant and unapologetic when describing his work, famously saying that Americans had only themselves to blame for the impact of misinformation in their lives (Smith & Banic, 2016). More distressing, however, is the fear that Dimitri is far from alone. In the time since *Fact vs. Fiction* was published, stories about the disinformation industries in Eastern Europe (Center for Media, Data and Society, 2020) and Russia (Allyn, 2020) in particular have become all too familiar, bringing with them acceptance of the idea that we're under attack by a nameless, nefarious army of genius coders who have learned to game a system few of us can even understand. In this scenario, we as information consumers are depicted as both blameless and helpless—neither of which is true. "Still," we're often asked, "who would do such a thing? Why would they?"

The motivations of people who create and share false information online are varied and complex. It's true, there are plenty of Dimitris in the world whose survival is linked to the financial incentives available to them as false content creators. However, they are just one piece of a much bigger puzzle. Moreover, there are others who benefit from a laser focus on the Dimitris of the world, because if we're only looking at Dimitri, that means we're not looking at them.

Misinformation, Disinformation, and Malinformation

The terms **misinformation** and **disinformation** are often used interchangeably, but they aren't the same. Understanding the difference can also help us understand the motivations of those who create or share each. *Mis*information refers to false information that is spread without the initial intent to deceive. Here's an example: "In the chaotic hours after the earthquake, a lot of misinformation was reported in the news." In this example, false information was generated and shared, but without the intention to cause harm. *Dis*information, by contrast, is false information that is deliberately misleading or manipulated. An example might be: "The politician purposely shared a hoax video that spread disinformation because they knew it would spark public outrage." While both misinformation and disinformation result in false content being spread, the motivations for each are very different (Wardle & Derakhshan, 2017). Finally, **malinformation** refers to information that is based in truth but that has been altered either in content or context to cause harm. Here's an example: "By changing the date of the photo, the online troll used malinformation to convince viewers that a long-ago event occurred

MIS   DIS   MAL
Information created and shared...

- Before all the facts are known
- Without knowing it is false

- With knowledge of inaccuracies/manipulation
- With the intention to deceive
- With acceptance of potential harm

- With intentional blending of factual information with known inaccuracies or manipulation
- With factual content presented out of context with the intention to deceive
- With intent to cause harm

Figure 4.1 The three types of false content differ in the creator's (or sharer's) motivation.

more recently." In this instance, the context is changed in order to mislead, but malinformation also refers to when the content itself is altered to cause harm, as well as the practice of adding true information to false content in order to cause harm. One example would be adding an individual's name and address to content that falsely implies that they are guilty of a serious crime or some other terrible act. While the crime may be real and the personal information shared may also be accurate, when combined, they create a false context that causes harm. These distinctions are important because they can help us understand the motivations of the people behind each type of false information (Figure 4.1).

But What About Bots?

In late 2020, researchers at the University of Southern California isolated thousands of automated accounts, or bots, on Twitter posting information related to the upcoming election. Headlines like "Twitter Bots Poised to Spread Disinformation Before Election" from *The New York Times* (Metz, 2020), while technically correct, add to the idea that the spread of disinformation is both inevitable and somehow detached from individuals. We see a danger in severing bots from their human creators. As computer scientist Kate Starbird wrote for the journal *Nature*, "Effective disinformation campaigns involve diverse participants; they might even include a majority of 'unwitting agents' who are unaware of their role, but who amplify and embellish messages that polarize communities and sow doubt about science, mainstream journalism and Western governments" (2019). We see the connection between the proliferation of mis-, dis-, and malinformation and human behavior as being empowering. After all, if the problem is ultimately our own creation, so too must be its solution.

Teach This Lens: Motives

This is why the final lens through which Digital Detectives *must* examine information is the Motives Lens. This lens requires Digital Detectives to consider the human behind the information they consume and how their motivations affect their decisions as content creators. Before trusting, sharing, or otherwise endorsing information they find online, Digital Detectives must first ask themselves a series of questions:

1. What do I know about the person/group sharing this information?
2. What behavior is this creator hoping this content will illicit?
3. Who benefits if I trust or share this information without digging deeper into its credibility?

Answers to these questions can help Digital Detectives develop questions to guide their deeper investigation into suspect information. (Check the **Digital Detective's Evidence Locker** for an infographic to help learners further understand this lens.)

Whether we're helping a group of fifth-grade students sharpen their skills as Digital Detectives, or we're working with their teachers to support them in developing curricula for the same purpose, we find that "lineup" activities are incredibly powerful. Lineups personalize the perpetrators of mis-, dis-, and malinformation and help learners build context for spotting their work.

Digital Detectives Know the Usual Suspects

As part of the process of applying the Four Lenses, we ask Digital Detectives to examine a group of suspects. Based on the evidence turned up by their investigations, we challenge them to match those details to the suspect who is most likely to have perpetrated the false information. While the word *fun* is rarely associated with information literacy, in our experience, these activities are exactly that. Learners of all ages get a kick out of trying to figure out the "whodunit" of mis-, dis-, or malinformation. What's more, we have found that understanding the preferred motives and tactics of specific suspects only adds to a Digital Detective's ability to spot them in use. Table 4.1 presents just a few of the suspects we've identified.

Table 4.1 The Digital Detective's Mug Book

SUSPECT	Motives
Click Chaser	• Fame! The Click Chaser is ready for their close-up! • Recognition • Their sole purpose is to get attention.
	Related to
	• Influencer for Hire • Spark • Wannabe

Tools and Tactics

- Potpourri! Click Chasers will use any tool at their disposal to get us to click, but especially…
- Sensational headlines
- Clickbait wording such as "You won't believe!" and "Shocking!"
- Emotional triggers, especially those that spark surprise, fear, and curiosity
- They often latch onto trending hashtags, even if their content isn't related.

Wins	Losses
• Clicks • Viral content • Attention (positive or negative) • Increased engagement • Growing like/share counts	• Silence • Lack of engagement

SUSPECT  **Troll**	**Motives**
	• To cause harm • Desire to divide, diminish, and destroy • Revenge • For trolls, this is personal.
	Related to
	• Outsider • Stan • Scaremonger

Tools and Tactics

- Bullying techniques
- Personal attacks
- Sensational language

- Emotional triggers, especially those that trigger hate, biases, or prejudice

Wins	**Losses**
• Attention • "Cancel culture" • Viral response • Validation from community	• Silence • Lack of engagement • Kindness

SUSPECT **Jokester**	**Motives**
	• Humor • Creativity • Curiosity ("Can this go viral?")
	Related to
	• Influencer for Hire • Spark • Click Chaser • *(Find out more about this suspect in the **Digital Detective's Evidence Locker**!)*

Tools and Tactics

- Satire
- Memes
- Obviously "faked" content
- Trends

- Celebrity support
- Emotional triggers, especially those that spark a feeling of superiority or amazement

Wins	**Losses**
• Positive engagement • Attention • Recognition • Viral content	• Negative engagement • Silence • Lack of engagement

SUSPECT — Influencer For Hire

Motives

- Money
- Sponsored content
- Brand association (the desire to be associated with a specific brand in a positive way)

Related to

- Click Chaser
- Spark
- Wannabe

Tools and Tactics

- Edited images and videos featuring products
- Personal endorsements and testimonials: "This product worked so well for me! You will love it!"
- Emotional triggers, especially those that spark a feeling of envy or personal empowerment
- Subtle (sometimes difficult-to-spot) references to ads/sponsorship

Wins

- Clicks
- Positive engagement, especially with a brand
- Growing like/share counts
- More sponsors

Losses

- Silence
- Lack of engagement
- Negative attention

SUSPECT — Propagandist

Motives

- Insurrection
- Political gain
- Interference in governance
- Anarchy

Related to

- Operative
- Sentry
- Insider

Tools and Tactics

- Edited content
- Advanced technology
- Sensational language
- Lots of layers; difficult to identify source
- Emotional triggers, especially those that spark fear, hate, and outrage

Wins

- Viral content
- Violence
- Public outrage
- Disruption of law and order
- Chaos

Losses

- Transparency/exposure
- Silence
- Lack of engagement

SUSPECT

Blue Liar

Motives

- Cousin to the White Liar. They spread false information because they believe the ends justify the means.
- Ultimate goal is societal change.
- Believe they are fighting for the "greater good"

Related to

- Click Chaser
- Insider
- Operative
- *(Find out more about this suspect in the **Digital Detective's Evidence Locker**!)*

Tools and Tactics

- Edited content or context to warn of a terrible outcome or event if something isn't prevented
- Sensational language
- Quotes from anonymous but official-sounding sources
- Emotional triggers, especially those that spark fear

Wins

- Public behavior changes
- Policy changes
- Viral content

Losses

- Lack of engagement
- Status quo

SUSPECT

Bot

Motives

- Surface motive is to spread increased engagement.
- Underlying motive is whatever drives the code writer that creates the program.
- Some bots are used to spread propaganda or other content. Others are used to make it seem as though an account has more engagement than it actually does (by boosting like, share, and follower numbers).

Related to

- Sock Puppet
- Cyborg
- Mimicker

Tools and Tactics

- Repetition: Most obvious bots will post hundreds of times a day.
- Cloning: User names may be similar but with numeric markers added.
- Sensational language/clickbait
- Outrageous claims with little evidence
- Emotional triggers, especially those that spark fear, hate, and outrage

Wins

- Viral content
- Increased engagement

Losses

- Blocks
- Account suspension
- Transparency when source is revealed

SUSPECT — Mimicker

Motives

- Create accounts and platforms to make false content appear as legitimate as possible by closely modeling trusted sources
- Make disinformation appear trustworthy

Related to

- Bot
- Doppelgänger
- Stan

Tools and Tactics

- Edited content
- Advanced technology to create content that looks/feels real
- Bot-like use of social media to automate the spread of content
- Emotional triggers, any and all

Wins

- Fool public
- Content recognized/shared as legitimate
- Viral content

Losses

- Transparency/exposure
- Labeled as "fake"
- Silence
- Lack of engagement

SUSPECT — Flash Bomber

Motives

- Distraction
- Draw attention away from another person or event
- Confusion and attention fatigue

Related to

- Spark
- Wannabe

Tools and Tactics

- Repetition: cluttering feeds with an overwhelming amount of information
- Sensational language/clickbait
- Outrageous claims coupled with emotionally charged media (such as photos or videos)
- Memes: easy-to-digest content
- Emotional triggers, especially those that spark fear, hate, outrage, or a feeling of being superior to those featured in the content

Wins

- Attention is drawn away from something else
- Public disengagement with news/information
- Public feeling that they are helpless to affect information feeds

Losses

- Silence
- Increased/sustained engagement on *other* content

SUSPECT	Motives
Lemming	• They just want to fit in. • Everyone else is sharing this, so should I! • The desire to belong and/or feel part of an important moment or movement
	Related to
	• Wannabe • Click Chaser • Stan

Tools and Tactics

- Sharing information without reading/vetting in order to be a part of a trend or movement
- Cloning: copying/sharing content from another source
- Hashtag floods (filling their posts, feeds, and comments with trending hashtags)
- Account bio/name changes to align with trends

Wins	Losses
• Positive attention • Recognition for engagement • Others follow their lead.	• Silence • Lack of engagement

In the **Digital Detective's Evidence Locker**, you'll find a complete list of suspect lineup cards, along with several ways to use them with learners of all ages.

Spend even a little time exploring the list of suspects who are most often responsible for creating and spreading false content, and some striking similarities begin to appear. As we've noted above, many of our suspects are related insomuch as they have similar goals or rely on parallel tactics to accomplish their goals. With this in mind, we created a family tree (Figure 4.2) to help Digital Detectives visualize these relationships.

We organized our tree based on the motivations of the suspects as well as on their own, likely, self-perceptions. However, we love it when Digital Detectives create their own "suspect family trees" based on other criteria or discoveries. In the **Digital Detective's Evidence Locker**, you'll find both a high-resolution version of our tree and a blank version that you can use to help your learners make connections about the behaviors that motivate

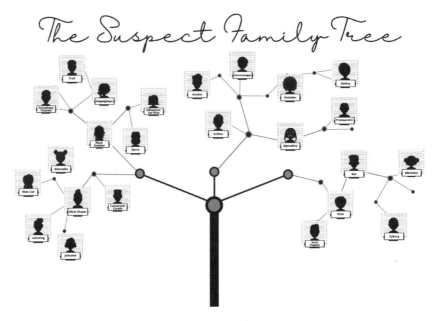

Figure 4.2 Motivations link the suspects in this family tree.

people to create and spread mis-, dis-, and malinformation. These connections can be powerful in part because, even though none of us would ever knowingly spread false content, all of us can relate to the emotions that drive others to do so. This understanding of harmful behavior doesn't excuse it. It does, however, help us become better at recognizing and avoiding it, essentially activating our "detective senses."

What We Do Next

As we've mentioned elsewhere in this book, the shift to a click-driven revenue system for journalists, in which they must produce viral content in order to stay solvent, has had far-reaching and enduring consequences, both for their profession and for our society. In this environment, the race to be first sometimes supersedes the race to be the best or the most accurate, which means even the most ethical, most trustworthy sources of information sometimes get it wrong. And of course, this means that *we* sometimes get it wrong.

Even the smartest, most reliable and honest people in your networks and timelines sometimes get triggered, duped, and fooled. What matters most in these situations is what we do next. Finding that an individual or group has spread misinformation doesn't necessarily make them a bad actor with nefarious intentions that we should never, ever trust again. Put the Motives Lens to work, ask questions, and look for evidence, especially when false content comes from an unexpected place.

- Has the source shared a public, transparent retraction or clarification? If sources simply delete their posts or never address their error, this is a red flag. However, if they acknowledge what happened and give additional context or updated information, that's a sign that the initial fumble was just that: a mistake they care about and wish to avoid in the future.

- How does the source react when questioned or called out? If sources ignore criticism or meet it with attacks of their own, that too is a credibility red flag. However, if they apologize, acknowledge the frustration of those who have come to trust and rely on them and/or share the standard they aspire to live up to, those are signs that they are working to do better.

What happens if *you* are the source of misinformation? Fairly or not, educators are held to an incredibly high standard in all areas of life, which includes their online activities. That doesn't, however, mean that you are perfect. If you find yourself in a situation in which you've unintentionally shared false information, a best practice is not only to acknowledge what happened but also think of it as a learning opportunity. Be transparent about why you shared the information to begin with. If that includes admitting that you were triggered by the content or that you didn't read or view the content fully before sharing it, own up to those missteps. Then share the process of discovering your mistake, learning the facts related to the content and your takeaways from the situation. Not only does this model best practices for those in your network, but it also reinforces the idea that we all make mistakes.

We're Only Human

Identifying suspects becomes easier work when we focus on the human behavior that underpins the digital results we encounter online and on our phones. Of the spread of disinformation, Tom Rosenstiel wrote, "[it's] not like a plumbing problem you fix. It is a social condition, like crime, that you must constantly monitor and adjust to" (as quoted in Anderson & Rainie, 2017). Although we're tempted to invoke some other plumbing-related metaphors here, this is the point we really want to focus on: behind every avatar, account name, verified blue check mark, and top commenter, there's a human creating content based on how they hope other humans will react. It's true, the tools and platforms through which mis-, dis-, and malinformation are created and spread are constantly changing. We can't possibly keep up with every new app and operating system. But human behavior is remarkably predictable. Proliferators of false content count on their ability to anticipate ours. It's our job to become better at recognizing theirs.

Terms of Detection

Disinformation: False information that is deliberately misleading or manipulated.

Malinformation: Information that is based in truth but that has been altered either in content or context to cause harm.

Misinformation: False information that is spread without the initial intent to deceive.

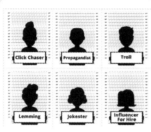

Suspect Lineup Activities

This Lens in Action:
Mini-Lessons to Try Tomorrow

Check the section tab marked Chapter 4 in the **Digital Detectives Evidence Locker** for a number of mini-lessons (ML) to help Digital Detectives sharpen their skills related to the Triggers Lens. Some examples include:

● Mobile vs. Traditional: Compare and Contrast Activities
● Digital Detective's Suspect Lineup Activities
● Digital Detective's Suspect "Head's Up" Games
● Plus more!

The Littlest Detectives: Strategies for K–3 Learners

Reminder: A variety of resources related to this chapter can be found in the **Digital Detective's Evidence Locker**. Use the QR code to the left or visit evidencelocker.online, then navigate to Chapter 5.

> The child is endowed with unknown powers, which can guide us to a radiant future. If what we really want is a new world, then education must take as its aim the development of these hidden possibilities.
>
> —Maria Montessori

What About the Littles?

We frequently receive requests for resources and information literacy lesson ideas that apply to younger learners. Primary grade teachers rightfully know that a child's understanding of deception and how to influence someone else's thinking begins around age 4 (Rhodes, 2017). Many see this developmental stage and the ones that follow as opportunities to help our youngest learners begin their journey as Digital Detectives but are unsure how to tackle this work with learners who are still mastering the building blocks of reading and math. In so many ways, those first few years of school form a foundation that will influence the rest of a child's life as a learner and human. That said, while the trend in U.S. education policy over the last several decades has been to create a more academic experience for primary grade students, our approach to information literacy for the littlest Digital Detectives leans more heavily into the developmental and social-emotional needs of learners at that age.

As we emphasize throughout this book, we believe that the problem of false information has less to do with the technology that amplifies it and is far more influenced by what *we* bring to the table as humans who are easily guided by our emotions. With this in mind, we see the primary grades as fertile ground for helping learners develop dispositions and habits that will make applying the Four Lenses more comfortable and more natural later on. Just as we help "littles" build habits around taking turns, sharing, and washing their hands, so too must we help them develop information literacy dispositions: habits that will help them grow into the best Digital Detectives possible. We've identified three critical dispositions that we feel are vital to this work.

Disposition 1: Connecting Information to Emotions

In Chapter 1, we unpacked how our emotional response to information drives our urge to trust and share it, while also influencing our decisions of what that information tells us. One of the reasons traditional information literacy efforts often fail is they lack a connection to social-emotional learning. The primary grades offer us an opportunity to help learners develop the habit of asking questions like "How does this make me feel?" when encountering new information or media. However, before this can happen, as educators, we have to broaden the idea of what "media" is. For our youngest learners, media may refer to any or all of the following:

- Picture books (explored independently or as part of a read-aloud)
- Classroom posters
- Images on a T-shirt
- Comics
- Television
- Movies

- ♀ Online video
- ♀ Music
- ♀ Games (board or video)

You get the picture. While our primary learners do come in contact with news, most of the media they consume doesn't fall into categories that we use for traditional information literacy instruction. However, all media sources have the potential to trigger an emotional response, which provides us with an opportunity for meaningful learning.

Imagine for a moment a group of first graders gathered (physically or virtually) for a read-aloud of Kate Hoefler and Corinna Luyken's 2020 picture book, *Nothing in Common*. Pages 5 and 6 of that book contain a spread featuring two kids watching an old man handing out flyers depicting his lost dog. It's a natural place to pause in the story and give kids time to look more closely at the illustrations, while you ask questions to keep them engaged. However, instead of asking comprehension questions here, such as "What's happening in this picture?" we suggest questions like, "How does this make you feel?" From there, a conversation about what they see happening in the artwork might naturally occur, but giving kids the space and time to sit with their emotions for a moment and then to articulate those feelings with others is important and allows their thinking to blossom. A year later, those same learners, now in second grade, might be asked a follow-up question like, "What action does that feeling make you want to take?" From there, conversations around good versus bad choices will come naturally. While related to the text, these same questions are also remarkably important to the process of evaluating the information these same learners will encounter online in just a few short years. By getting them in the habit of asking these types of questions now, we are essentially prepping the ground for later harvest.

If we want learners to develop the habit of thinking about how information triggers emotion, then we must, in turn, develop some instructional habits of our own. Intentionally creating opportunities for questioning that allows kids to pause, make connections, and reflect on those ideas, throughout an instructional day and across subject areas, requires planning. Whether students are watching a YouTube video for a PE lesson or taking a virtual field trip to the moon for science, reserving a few minutes for those learners to consider how the information they just consumed made them feel is necessary. *Kids recognize repetition and emphasis as value statements.* When we repeatedly model a strategy, they begin to recognize it as something we value. Practice across disciplines only reinforces the idea that this type of reflection is important.

Questions to Try Tomorrow

When combined with information consumption, be it a picture book or a video, all of the questions in Table 5.1 help learners draw connections between information and emotion. Whether the emotions are positive or negative, this simple act helps kids develop the habit of thinking metacognitively about how information triggers emotional responses. This reflection adds new layers to the way they perceive the world and their place in it.

Table 5.1 Questions to Try Tomorrow

Grades	Question	Action
K+	How does _____ make you feel?	Ask learners to think about and identify their own emotional responses.
1st +	How does _____ emotion feel in/to your body?	Ask learners to connect emotion to physical responses. Examples might be: feeling nervous, "butterflies in the stomach," sweating, fidgety, tired, and so on.
2nd+	What action does this emotion make you want to take?	Ask learners to connect emotion to decision-making.
3rd +	What are some ways to calm strong emotions?	Ask learners to identify healthy ways to relieve emotional stress and/or anxiety.

Likert Scales

Likert Scales are simple tools that help people rate the strength of a feeling toward something. Questions that begin with "On a scale of 1–5, how strongly do you agree or disagree with . . ." are familiar uses of Likert Scales. With a little modification, however, Likert Scales can be valuable in helping younger learners think about the intensity of their emotional response to something, too. Visual Likert Scales, like Figure 5.1, are an example of how these tools can be used to help young learners both identify emotions and consider how strong those emotions are.

Figure 5.1 Use a visual Likert Scale like this one to help young learners communicate their emotional reactions.

Consider our previous example of students responding to questions about how illustrations in a picture book make them feel: Using a Likert Scale like this, teachers could approach this moment in a different way. They could ask learners to place a dot under the image that best captures their emotional reaction to the text, allowing each child to interpret the star ratings in their own way. For slightly older learners, once the emotion is identified, a scale like the one above can be used to help them describe how strong the feeling is. Throughout the unit plans in Chapters 8, 9, and 10, we used Likert Scales with learners of all ages. Any of those examples, as well as the mini-lessons from the lens-specific chapters, could be tweaked for use with younger kids.

Disposition 2: Curiosity

In Chapter 3, we explored the ways that traditional information literacy models must evolve away from simple checklists and toward authentic, inquiry-driven investigations. Rather than asking learners to check off boxes on a list, we encourage educators to coach students as they develop questions that guide their own inquiries. These investigations should be rooted in the credibility red flags that they discover along the way but should also be equally inspired by their own curiosities. When we work with students (and teachers), we find that this shift from identifying to investigating is sometimes the biggest hurdle for both to jump. At the same time, it is also the most important. As the Long Island Explorium proclaims, "The future belongs to the curious. The ones who are not afraid to try it, explore it, poke at it, question it and turn it inside out."

A focus on standardized testing has created instructional environments where many kids (and adults!) are highly motivated to turn every task into one that results in a single, static, correct answer. However, information literacy doesn't work like that. As we try to make clear in the unit plans that follow in Chapters 8, 9, and 10, the final verdict in a case is often not cut-and-dried. Rather than asking learners to label information *true* or *false*, we ask them to think about whether the information is credible enough to trust and share. This type of ambiguity can be frustrating for kids (and adults) who've come to expect consistently concrete outcomes from learning. However, this cognitive flexibility is a necessary component of a Digital Detective's work. The primary grades offer an opportunity to create instructional environments that help learners not only become more comfortable with uncertainty but also to recognize ambiguity as inspiration for curiosity.

This Is Your Brain on Curiosity

The idea that curiosity makes learning more effective and enjoyable is not new. Decades of research underscores what great teachers have always known: Curious students not only ask questions but also actively seek out the answers. Most importantly, they relish the process. Here are just a few ways that curiosity enhances learning:

- ♀ **Curiosity prepares the brain for learning.** Research reveals that curiosity about a topic activates the portions of the brain that make learning easier. Curiosity is like the brain's wake-up call, signaling our brains to get ready for action (Gruber et al., 2014)!

- ♀ **Curiosity makes learning sticky.** Researchers have observed that when curiosity is the motivation for learning, that learning is retained for much longer than the stuff we learn because we have to. Information gained through curiosity-powered learning gets moved from temporary to permanent storage (Yuhas, 2014).

- ♀ **Curiosity makes future learning more rewarding.** Researchers have found that when curiosity is activated, our brains get a shot of dopamine, a chemical that signals pleasure. Over time, we learn to associate curiosity-driven learning with joy (Gruber et al., 2014).

Making Curiosity a Habit

Helping students grow into curious thinkers, who approach the work of learning comfortable with uncertainty and excited to explore uncharted territories, requires practice. Some ways to build these opportunities into the instructional day are to:

- ♀ **Connect curiosity to academic learning.** Pure exploration time is wonderful, but connecting those investigations to "serious learning" helps students see curiosity as part of the learning process, rather than something extra that we do only when time allows (Table 5.2).

Table 5.2 Activities to Connect Creativity and Learning

Grade	Activity	Curiosity Boosted!
1st	Planting beans and watching them grow up a stalk in order to observe the life cycle of a plant.	• In the days ahead, reveal one or two of the materials that will be used. Let kids explore and make predictions about what they're about to do. • Grow a second stalk in which kids get to make decisions about cultivating the plants based on their "what-ifs?"
3rd	Using a graphic organizer to separate factual statements from opinions.	• Rather than giving students the fact/opinion statements to sort, have them explore a website like Wonderopolis.org to decide on a topic to focus on. • Then have students create their own fact/opinion statements about the wonder they explored. Note: If your third graders aren't ready to write down those statements, they can record them using a tool like Flipgrid. • Later, have them use the graphic organizer to sort their classmates' statements into different categories.

🔑 **Reward curiosity.** Just as we reward kids (with everything from praise to prizes) for finding the right answer, build in rewards for kids whose curiosity is taking shape. Acknowledging great questions, creating bulletin boards that capture exceptional wonderings, and pausing a lesson to both find and share the answer to a student's query are all ways to show learners that you value their questions and that curiosity isn't a distraction *from* learning, it's fuel *for* learning!

🔑 **Model your own curiosity.** Curiosity may have killed the cat, but it's an essential component of learning. Great teachers model what it means to be a lifelong learner, joyful reader, or productive citizen because they understand that kids need to see examples of what we say we want them to become. Making your internal wonderings public throughout the instructional day helps kids see what a curious mind looks like. Adding phrases like, "Hmmmm. I wonder what might happen if I click here?!" or "This makes me want to learn more about this artist/author/scientist to conversations with young learners and to the ways we introduce material are both examples of how to model curiosity for kids.

Disposition 3: Empathy

First, empathy is about noticing: noticing that the world affects some people differently than it does others, noticing that our own actions affect others, noticing that we have the power to mitigate or intensify those effects. Then, empathy demands that we do more than care. Empathy demands that we act in ways that demonstrate compassion. As Chad C. Everett explained, "The end point of empathy is not feeling. The true end point of empathy is action" (2017).

In Chapter 4, we took a deep dive into how understanding the motivations of those creating false information can help us recognize their work and guide our own decisions as Digital Detectives. Although we don't think young learners are ready to start thinking about suspects and cases, we know they are ready to start noticing the world around them and how others are affected by it. By acting as coaches in the art of noticing, primary grade teachers, librarians, and others who support these little learners have the opportunity to help them develop habits that can lead to empathetic actions later. Digital Detective work is inextricably linked to empathy in the way that it requires us to think not only about how information makes us feel, but also about how it makes others feel and how our decisions to trust and share false content affect others. Our littlest learners can begin their journey as Digital Detectives first by building the habit of noticing, but only if we create spaces and instruction that connect them with that world.

The Danger of a Single Story

Chimamanda Ngozi Adichie's 2009 TEDGlobal Talk, "The Danger of a Single Story," explores the way that narrative shapes our beliefs about people and cultures. Adichie warns that exposure to narratives that present only one view of people who look and live differently from ourselves results in opinions and biases about them that are, at best, incomplete and, at worst, harmful. When we work with educators to design information literacy programs in their schools or districts, we often ask them to watch Adichie's lecture alongside Eli Pariser's 2011 TED Talk, "Beware Online 'Filter Bubbles,'" with the challenge of then describing how the two are related. As the conversation evolves, it becomes clear that these are parallel messages. Our online lives represent a narrative that is heavily influenced by filter bubbles, forming a "single story." And single stories result in views that can cause harm.

We believe in surrounding learners of all ages with inclusive stories that present multiple narratives about people and the lives they lead. However, it's not hard to argue that this work is especially important in the primary grades. While the work of learning to read is often seen as the essential function of elementary school, we believe that the work of *reading to learn* (about the world, its people, and our place in it) is just as vital. In the primary grades, we have the opportunity to use story as a tool for helping learners develop the habit of noticing those things while simultaneously developing rich, joyful reading identities.

Books Everywhere

Books are empathy-building machines. Research has confirmed that reading about other people helps us imagine ourselves in their position, which then enables us to better understand people and empathize with them. We believe picture books are a uniquely effective tool for helping kids develop both the habit of noticing and the elusive ability to empathize with others. In the **Digital Detective's Evidence Locker**, we've curated a list of picture books that we recommend for this work. Some are related to information literacy, but many are related to the art of noticing the world and thinking about our place

in it. We decided to put the bulk of this list in the Evidence Locker because we hope to keep adding to it, but a few of our favorites at the time of this publication are listed in Table 5.3.

Table 5.3 Books to Build Empathy

Title	Creators	Date Published
Nana Akua Goes to School	Tricia Elam Walker (Author) April Harrison (Illustrator)	2020
We Are Water Protectors	Carole Lindstrom (Author) Michaela Goade (Illustrator)	2020
Julián Is a Mermaid	Jessica Love (Author, Illustrator)	2018
Eyes That Kiss in the Corners	Joanna Ho (Author) Dung Ho (Illustrator)	2020
Milo Imagines the World	Matt de la Peña (Author) Christian Robinson (Illustrator)	2021
Our Little Kitchen	Jillian Tamaki (Author, Illustrator)	2020
Nothing in Common	Kate Hoefler (Author) Corinna Luyken (Illustrator)	2020
Lubna and Pebble	Wendy Meddour (Author) Daniel Egnéus (Illustrator)	2019
I Talk Like a River	Jordan Scott (Author) Sydney Smith (Illustrator)	2020
Your Name Is a Song	Jamilah Thompkins-Bigelow (Author) Luisa Uribe (Illustrator)	2020
I See. I See.	Robert Henderson (Author, Illustrator)	2019
Woodpecker Girl	Chingyen Liu and I-Tsun Chiang (Authors) Heidi Doll (Illustrator)	2020

However, buying these books, and countless others, is only the first step. These books must be shared with learners, first by displaying them and then through book talks and read-alouds. From school libraries to classrooms filled with bookshelves, from collections of picture books in the principal's office to books lining the walls of the cafeteria, physical schools should be a visual representation of the power of story. Then it's up to every adult in the building to share those stories with learners.

Pairing a picture book with academic content that affords kids a glimpse into a world or experience that is different from their own offers us the opportunity to practice empathy skills. Every content area contains these connection points. While classroom teachers and coaches are experts at locating those places in the content that lend themselves to this work, your school librarian is ready to help you match the moment with the right picture book. This powerful duo can create magic for little learners who will one day be ready to earn their Digital Detective's badges.

Inclusivity Everywhere

One thing you may have noticed about the list of picture books that we shared is that even our small collection of recommendations features stories and authors representing an array of diverse cultures and experiences. This is by design. Building collections of stories that power empathy means an intentional focus on inclusivity to ensure that our learners engage with multiple, varied narratives about different experiences in order to help them notice what life is like for people who look and live differently from how they do.

This same philosophy applies to the digital resources we share and the images we use to convey our school community. As Katie Muhtaris and Kristin Ziemke explained in their book, *Read the World*, "Technology brings us an infinite number of bits of information, but human beings do not understand the world in terms of bits of information. Instead, we shape those bits of information into stories. Story links information to emotion and creates meaning" (2019, p. 7). When we build websites or collections of resources for parents and kids in which all the people depicted look the same, we are creating a "single story" about our community which, at best, is incomplete.

Kids internalize these messages, even if we didn't intend to send them. What's more, these internalized messages are later used to divide people into categories based on limited and perhaps even faulty understanding. With that in mind, we must make sure that the messages we're sending are the ones we really want kids to notice and reflect on.

Digital Detectives in Training

Our littlest learners are not ready to apply the Four Lenses to the information they consume. They do consume information, however, and they *are* ready to start developing dispositions that will help prepare them for the work that lies ahead. When today's youngest learners are signing up for their first account on whatever platform is their equivalent to Snapchat or TikTok, we want to make sure that they're already in the habit of considering how information makes them feel. We want those same learners to not need prompting to notice how information may affect others. And we need them to know how to use curiosity to investigate further. While information literacy work may seem like it's best suited to tweens, teens, and adults, this work actually begins with our littlest learners and with the educators whose job it is to help them grow into exceptional humans.

The Digital Detective Squad

 **Reminder:** A variety of resources related to this chapter can be found in the **Digital Detective's Evidence Locker**. Use the QR code to the left or visit evidencelocker.online, then navigate to Chapter 6.

> What you believe about the future will change how you live in the present.
>
> —Daniel Nayeri

One of the most interesting parts of this journey for us has been asking others what comes to mind when they hear the term *Digital Detective*. The answers we've received have been varied and inspiring. Some people have responded with visions of old-school, Baker Street–style detectives whose magnifying glasses have been replaced by a digital device. Others say the term conjures images of coded androids seeking out and destroying disinformation with laser-like truth blasts. Our friend Jarrett Lerner (who created all the Finish This Comic! activities in the **Digital Detective's Evidence Locker**) also created Figure 6.1 in response to that question, which we love. In the Evidence Locker, you'll find an activity for kids in Chapter 6 that asks them to do this very thing: draw or create what they think a Digital Detective looks like. We see this as both a wonderful pre- and post-assessment that gives kids a chance to make predictions, think creatively, and synthesize what they've learned.

Of course, we've got our own ideas about what a Digital Detective looks like, but what's most important to us is that these imaginings are rooted in the habits that guide a Digital Detective's work. While the ways in which each of the following are demonstrated across grade levels will vary, we believe that the following attributes are fundamental to the identity of the Digital Detective:

- *Digital Detectives* think critically about how information affects themselves and others.
- *Digital Detectives* are curious questioners who feel empowered to follow their own investigative inquiries.
- *Digital Detectives* make evidence- and empathy-driven decisions about the information they trust and share.
- *Digital Detectives* model these practices for others.

Figure 6.1 What do you think a Digital Detective looks like? Jarrett Lerner offers one idea.

In the days ahead, as you work with students and perhaps even colleagues, these attributes (among others you may identify as important to your specific context) will be things to look for as you decide whether your learners have earned their (figurative or literal) Digital Detective's badges. In the Evidence Locker for this chapter, you'll find a series of digital badges that you can use with learners of all ages, if you choose. Among them, you'll find a unique badge for educators like yourself who have read the book and who are ready to lead in the work ahead. We're counting on you.

Squad Goals

One of our goals for this book is to serve as a conduit not just between educators and information but also as one that connects educators to one another. We have no doubt that as you implement our resources and lessons in classrooms and libraries with your students, you'll think of ways to improve upon them. What's more, we're hoping that you'll be inspired to design your own case files and lens-specific activities that you'll want to share with others who are tackling this work. In short, we want you as a member of our Digital Detective Squad.

With that in mind, the **Digital Detective's Evidence Locker** for Chapter 6 includes a DIY Digital Detective Case section. In this space, you'll find instructions and tips for creating your own cases to use with kids. This section also provides you with tools for submitting and sharing your own lesson ideas with us. Those we select will be added to the Teacher-Created Resource section of the appropriate chapter. Additionally, we'll be using the hashtag #digitaldetectivesquad online to keep the conversation going and to share updates and resources. If you're active on social media, please join us there.

Being part of the Digital Detective Squad means both that you're modeling the attributes of a Digital Detective in your own online behavior and that you're willing to share ideas for helping students become Digital Detectives with others (Figure 6.2). If there's one thing we've learned about the work of information literacy, it's that we can't do it alone. We need each other.

The Hill We Climb

While Chapter 6 marks the end of the first section of this book, if we've done our job right, it will also represent the beginning of a new journey for you and the students you serve. While the chapters before this one are designed to support *you* as a learner, those that follow are all about implementation. We began this book with a set of core beliefs that served as the guiding principles of our work. The last of those beliefs was: *Our world needs digital detectives more than ever.* And that's true. But if we're really being honest, what our world might need even more right now is you!

Since this book opened with a quote from President Biden's inaugural address, it feels fitting to close this section with one from National Youth Poet Laureate Amanda Gorman's speech on the same day:

If we're to live up to our own time, then
        victory
Won't lie in the blade, but in all the bridges
        we've made.
That is the promised glade,
The hill we climb, if only we dare it. (2021, p. 19)

The work ahead requires daring and determination. Although we've laid a foundation for helping you get started, it will ultimately be up to you (and those you recruit to your own squad!) to make it happen.

Figure 6.2 We need to work together as a Digital Detective Squad.

If you'll allow your authors a personal note, we, like many of you, went into education with the desire to make the world better. Neither of us, however, could have envisioned that we'd spend the last five years chasing that goal by trying to improve information literacy instruction. We both became educators with different passions that we assumed would drive the rest of our careers. That said, while neither of us could have guessed that this is the path our journey would take us on, we both fervently believe that this is the most important work we can be doing right now. When working with educators, we often joke that we "doomscroll" for a living. And while there's some truth to that, the reality is that our job is about helping you change the world. We take that responsibility seriously, and we hope you find this book a useful tool in that pursuit.

Amanda Gorman's "The Hill We Climb" ends with the following lines:

> When day comes, we step out of the
>   shade,
> Aflame and unafraid.
> The new dawn blooms as we free it,
> For there is always light,
> If only we're brave enough to see it,
> If only we're brave enough to be it. (2021, p. 29)

We see that light in you. So, let's get to the work of being it! We look forward to connecting with you and cheering you on along the way.

Putting It All Together: How to Use the Unit Plans and Related Resources

Reminder: A variety of resources related to this chapter can be found in the **Digital Detective's Evidence Locker**. Use the QR code to the left or visit evidencelocker.online, then navigate to Chapter 7.

As previously mentioned, Chapters 8, 9, and 10 consist of unit plans designed to help learners assume the role of Digital Detective by applying the Four Lenses to a broad array of news stories from various information sources. One of our goals in creating these units was to build an instructional prototype that you can use straight from the book. With a little creativity, you can also easily adapt it if you identify necessary tweaks to meet your learners' unique needs. In this way, we see our plans as an instructional launchpad: Use them as-is for as long as you feel necessary, but when you are ready, feel free to build on them to create something even better.

So You Want to Be a Digital Detective, Eh?

Each unit plan has been framed as a case to be solved. Each case revolves around a few central mysteries: Can this information be trusted? Or, has it been manipulated or fabricated? And, if the latter is true, who is responsible for the deception? Of course, to solve those mysteries learners must answer other questions related to credibility and their own responsibility as both a

Digital Detective and as a human being living in an information-saturated world. Although cracking the case is one of the objectives that learners should strive for, the bigger goal is for them to think about how their own information transactions affect both their own well-being and that of those they are connected to. In the end, being a Digital Detective isn't only about collecting clues and discerning fact from fiction; it's also about using those skills to create and contribute to a better world.

Basic Structure

All of our unit plans follow a similar structure, regardless of the grade span for which they are intended. This structure is based on what we know about how humans consume and process information. For example, as mentioned previously, we know that people spend only about eight seconds (on average) evaluating a headline, image, or other snippets of information before making an initial judgment about its credibility. Because so much of that information is accessed through social media, which provides us with the instant ability to endorse and share it, the eight seconds we spend processing and evaluating content very often results in the algorithm-driven community spread. If in those eight seconds we decide to trust the content we've bumped up against, or our emotional response to it ignites the urge to pass it on, the single tap or click it takes to like or share that content and follow those who created it only increases the likelihood that many others will then spend eight seconds of their day doing the same.

Step 1: The Case One-Sheet

Those eight seconds, and the human tendency to engage with (and therefore endorse) information without fully vetting it, were the inspiration for the case one-sheet. While all unit plans offer suggestions for activating their prior knowledge related to the case, this single page, a visual-driven resource, is the first thing that should be given to learners as they begin their work as Digital Detectives (Figure 7.1). Although you will undoubtedly provide them with more than eight seconds to do it, the case one-sheet was designed to mimic the truncated way we evaluate information in the real world. This one-sheet is an opportunity for learners to create an initial hypothesis about the case based on limited information. By comparing these initial predictions to later determinations, learners can also reflect on how authentic, curiosity-driven investigations provide more clues and better tools for parsing credibility.

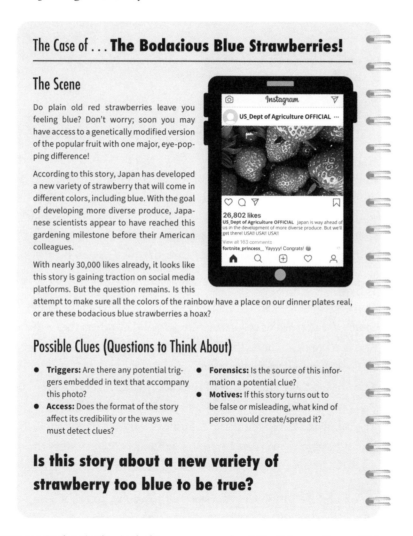

The Case of . . . **The Bodacious Blue Strawberries!**

The Scene

Do plain old red strawberries leave you feeling blue? Don't worry; soon you may have access to a genetically modified version of the popular fruit with one major, eye-popping difference!

According to this story, Japan has developed a new variety of strawberry that will come in different colors, including blue. With the goal of developing more diverse produce, Japanese scientists appear to have reached this gardening milestone before their American colleagues.

With nearly 30,000 likes already, it looks like this story is gaining traction on social media platforms. But the question remains. Is this attempt to make sure all the colors of the rainbow have a place on our dinner plates real, or are these bodacious blue strawberries a hoax?

Possible Clues (Questions to Think About)

- **Triggers:** Are there any potential triggers embedded in text that accompany this photo?
- **Access:** Does the format of the story affect its credibility or the ways we must detect clues?
- **Forensics:** Is the source of this information a potential clue?
- **Motives:** If this story turns out to be false or misleading, what kind of person would create/spread it?

Is this story about a new variety of strawberry too blue to be true?

Figure 7.1 Each unit plan includes a case one-sheet like this one. Present it to learners at the start of the unit plan.

Step 2: The Case File

Figure 7.2 You'll find the case file for each unit plan in the **Digital Detective's Evidence Locker**.

The **Digital Detective's Evidence Locker** (Figure 7.2) contains a *case file* for each unit plan. The case file includes links to resources that can be used to detect additional evidence and clues for solving the case. Some case files include red herrings, and many have tools and strategies for helping learners hone specific skills related to this case's credibility. After reviewing the case one-sheet and using it to form an initial hypothesis of the case, learners then explore the resources contained in the case file, which can be accessed in several ways:

- **The Digital Case File:** Using a tool such as Google Docs, Google Slides, Padlet, Wakelet, or any other digital curation tool, educators can create an online case file for learners to access remotely or use a digital device at school.
- **The Analog Case File:** Many of the case file resources can be printed and distributed to learners via an actual file folder.
- **The Gamified Case File:** Using a digital or physical Breakout EDU box, educators can create "brain break" tasks between steps that require learners to solve puzzles to access items from the case file.

However you choose to give learners access to the case file, it's important to note that these resources are divided into two categories in the Evidence Locker. Those in blue (online) represent potential evidence or clues but do not reveal the case (Figure 7.3). Those in red, by contrast, are spoilers. Think of

Case File

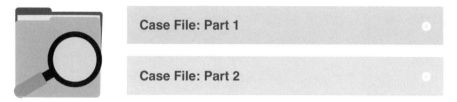

Figure 7.3 Resources in the blue category (shown here at the top [Part 1]) provide clues but do not reveal the case; those in the red (shown here at the bottom [Part 2]) are spoilers.

the resources in red as part of the answer key to the case. These should not be given to learners until later in the process (if at all).

One other thing to note about the case files: Each also contains a high-resolution version of the image shared in the case one-sheet. These higher-quality versions of a previously shared resource may allow learners to take a closer, more transparent, look at a piece of evidence. However, they may also be useful to the teacher who can display it (during either remote or face-to-face learning) for a whole group conversation about what learners first noticed. Additionally, a strategy like Written Conversations (see the **Digital Detective's Evidence Locker** for more information) can be used to document learners' initial wonderings and predictions about the case. This documentation can plant seeds for rich discussions later.

The Digital Detective's Notebook

Many unit plans also point to templates in the Digital Detective's Notebook that can help scaffold learning or document the journey learners take in processing the clues. While we recommend these worksheets for use with specific cases, they were designed with flexibility in mind. In addition to using them with any of the units in our book, you may find that you don't need to use them at all. The Digital Detective's Notebook (highlighted in purple in the Evidence Locker for Chapters 8, 9, and 10; Figure 7.4) mimics the notebook kept by all detectives: a resource for capturing clues and making notes

Digital Detective's Notebook

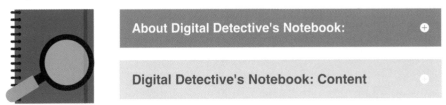

Figure 7.4 The Digital Detective's Notebook provides an opportunity for learners to capture and sort through clues and thoughts on the case.

for future reference. Ultimately, these resources were designed to scaffold learning, not to standardize it. We believe there is a value (both for learners and their teachers) in the processes captured in these worksheets, but we encourage you to be creative in the ways you implement them.

Digital Detective's Toolbox

In addition to the templates contained in the Digital Detective's Notebook, all of our unit plans reference digital tools or suggested instructional strategies for making Digital Detective work as meaningful and pedagogically rich as possible. These instructional resources are located in the green section of the Evidence Locker labeled the Digital Detective's Toolbox (Figure 7.5). Although you may share some of these resources with learners, they are not intended for inclusion in the case file.

Digital Detective's Toolbox

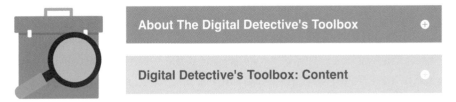

Figure 7.5 The Digital Detective's Toolbox contains suggested digital tools and instructional strategies to supplement the cases.

Step 3: The Facts of the Case

Once they have reviewed the case file, collected clues, and investigated the evidence, Digital Detectives should be ready to render a more information-based verdict in the case. Although we've included resources in the Evidence Locker to support this step, what matters most is that learners are given the opportunity to:

- Compare their conclusions to their initial hypothesis
- Use evidence from the case file to support their assertions

Once this is completed, it's time for you to reveal the facts of the case. Each unit plan contains an answer key called The Facts of the Case that classifies the clues and evidence into categories based on the Four Lenses while empha-sizing the most significant lens in detecting the credibility of this specific case. While these answer keys are robust, they are not comprehensive. As they gain skill as Digital Detectives, your learners are bound to identify addi-tional clues that we left out or point out ways that some clues may be applied to multiple lenses.

Step 4: Synthesis and Beyond!

In some ways, solving the case is just the first step toward more in-depth learning. We've designed each unit so that once the learners understand whether or not a story is credible, their job then shifts to applying that under-standing in two ways. They need to:

- Explore other possibilities that might not have been introduced by the authors or you, the teacher
- Help all the learners reflect on their responsibility as a human living in an information-rich world

To set the stage for what is ultimately the most crucial part of each unit, we begin each plan focusing on the Big Ideas. In this section, we invite you to think about the potential ripples your instruction may have on the world beyond your learning space. In the Introduction, we said we believe information literacy is the most important work we can be doing at this moment in history. It's going to take all of us, working together, to make a dent in the infodemic that continues to influence the decisions we make as citizens and humans. Given the sheer number of things you have to accomplish in a single day, it's easy to get lost in the details that crowd an instructional day. The Big Ideas section of each unit plan is designed to help all of us keep our eyes on the prize.

Similarly, the SEL Spotlight section at the beginning of each unit serves as a reminder of the important connection between this work and social-emotional learning (SEL). The Triggers Lens may not be the focus of every lesson, but our emotional response to information must always be on our radar so we will help our learners navigate an information landscape that relies on our clicks for its survival. As we unpacked in Chapter 3, our learners have not yet developed the gray matter necessary for consistent, careful, methodical thinking; it is our job to help them:

- Recognize red flags within the information they consume, such as clues that reveal emotional triggers were embedded within the information and clues that those triggers are influencing their urge to trust and share information
- Develop strategies for managing those emotional responses

The SEL Spotlight in each unit plan was also designed to align with the CASEL Framework and associated core competencies, emphasizing growth and self-management along the grade span continuum. Although your school or district may not be focusing on SEL at this time, we hope this alignment will help support this work within the context of news/information literacy.

Let's Get to Work!

The unit plans in the following chapters are the heart of this book. Although the lens-specific mini-lessons in Chapters 1 through 4 can stand alone to develop isolated skills or serve as scaffolds for skills that need reinforcing, their true purpose is to support the more robust and meaningful Digital Detective work the unit plans aspire to create. With this in mind, we encourage you to think outside the grade spans we've identified. For example, if you teach seventh grade, we hope you'll explore the cases designed for both elementary and high school learners, too. With your experience brought to bear, we're betting some of those lessons could be reworked for your Digital Detectives as well. Our fervent hope is that in the hands of creative educators, they can be wielded as tools for fighting mis-, dis-, and malinformation before it can take root. We look forward to seeing their future iterations as you build on what we've created and make it even better.

Digital Detective's Lessons for Elementary Age Learners

This chapter consists of four lessons designed to help elementary age learners assume the role of Digital Detectives by applying the Four Lenses to a broad array of news stories from various information sources.

These lessons are supported by tools and resources to help you implement them as soon as you feel your Digital Detectives are ready to start cracking cases. As noted earlier, we encourage you to think outside the grade spans we've identified. For example, if you teach elementary learners, we hope you'll explore the cases designed for both middle grade and high school learners, too. With your experience brought to bear, we're betting some of those lessons could be reworked for your Digital Detectives as well.

Contents

The Case of . . . **The Bodacious Blue Strawberries!**

The Scene

Do plain old red strawberries leave you feeling blue? Don't worry; soon you may have access to a genetically modified version of the popular fruit with one major, eye-popping difference!

According to this story, Japan has developed a new variety of strawberry that will come in different colors, including blue. With the goal of developing more diverse produce, Japanese scientists appear to have reached this gardening milestone before their American colleagues.

With nearly 30,000 likes already, it looks like this story is gaining traction on social media platforms. But the question remains. Is this attempt to make sure all the colors of the rainbow have a place on our dinner plates real, or are these bodacious blue strawberries a hoax?

Possible Clues (Questions to Think About)

- **Triggers:** Are there any potential triggers embedded in text that accompany this photo?
- **Access:** Does the format of the story affect its credibility or the ways we must detect clues?

- **Forensics:** Is the source of this information a potential clue?
- **Motives:** If this story turns out to be false or misleading, what kind of person would create/spread it?

Is this story about a new variety of strawberry too blue to be true?

💡 Big Ideas

This lesson focuses on the *Access* and *Triggers* Lenses. While the source of information is often not the last word in determining credibility (in today's fast-paced, click-driven information landscape, even the most reputable and ethical sources sometimes get things wrong), learning more about the person behind the information can help us better understand the motivations that guide their choices as a creator. In this case, the mobile device and app through which the information is accessed adds extra layers of complexity to this work. Ultimately, we want learners to think deeply about the clues that give us pause about the credibility of the source sharing the information. Despite the fact that the source identifies as an "official account," learners should have questions about whether or not the source's creative choices support that claim. The objectives below were created to help learners a) peel back the layers presented by mobile devices and social media that may stand between them and the source of the information they are consuming, and b) think deeply about how those layers might be used by nefarious actors to both deceive and influence us.

🦋 SEL Spotlight

Although this case is about a modified fruit, it could easily be used as a metaphor for the kids you teach. As your learners grow and their experiences with the world and other people (both online and in person) increase, so too does their awareness of how they fit into the larger world around them. Whether on the playground, in the cafeteria, or online, these interactions are opportunities for our kids to learn two important truths: They are unique and complex, and they are a part of a whole, a collective that is influenced and shaped by the actions of individuals.

CASEL defines social awareness as "the ability to take the perspective of and empathize with others, including those from diverse backgrounds and cultures" (2020). This definition includes such teachable skills as perspective-taking, empathy, appreciating diversity, and respect for others. The activities in this lesson provide a safe access point for learners to:

- ♀ Consider how different perspectives influence how different people perceive the same event in different ways
- ♀ Develop skills for using empathy to view information from a perspective that is different from their own
- ♀ Consider the ways that differing perspectives and opinions benefit us as a society
- ♀ Understand their responsibility as information consumers/creators in making sure that false information isn't spread under the guise of being an alternate perspective

Curricula Connections

Target Audience	4th–5th (As with all lessons in this book, this grade span is a suggestion only. With a few adaptations, this lesson could easily be introduced to other learners.)

Potential Content Area Connections/Collaborations

- Science: Color variants in foods, genetically modified foods
- Social Studies: History of competition between America and Japan

ISTE Standards

Students

- Knowledge Constructor (3b): Students evaluate the accuracy, perspective, credibility and relevance of information, media, data or other resources.
- Knowledge Constructor (3d): Students build knowledge by actively exploring real-world issues and problems, developing ideas and theories and pursuing answers and solutions.
- Creative Communicator (6c): Students communicate complex ideas clearly and effectively by creating or using various digital objects such as visualizations, models or simulations.
- Creative Communicator (6d): Students publish or present content that customizes the message and medium for their intended audiences.

Educators

- Citizen (3b): Educators establish a learning culture that promotes curiosity and critical examination of online resources and fosters digital literacy and media fluency.
- Citizen (3c): Educators mentor students in safe, legal and ethical practices with digital tools and protect intellectual rights and property.
- Designer (5b): Educators design authentic learning activities that align with content area standards and use digital tools and resources to maximize active, deep learning.
- Analyst (7a): Educators provide alternative ways for students to demonstrate competency and reflect on their learning using technology.

Learning Objectives

By the end of this lesson:

- The learner will apply the Four Lenses to information as a step in determining credibility.
- The learner will discover ways to identify "official" accounts on social media.
- The learner will explore ways in which images can be altered to fool viewers.
- The learner will understand the concept of hoax news.
- The learner will develop and share a hypothesis related to information credibility.
- The learner will synthesize learning by suggesting "official" social media accounts that could be followed by their teacher, librarian, or principal.

Resources Needed for This Lesson

Reminder: A variety of resources related to this chapter can be found in the Digital Detective's Evidence Locker. Use the QR code to the left, or visit evidencelocker.online. Then navigate to Chapter 8.

Time Needed for This Lesson: 2–4 hours

Case File

The following supplemental resources from the Digital Detective's Evidence Locker may be given to students to examine the case:

- [IMAGE] Hi-res version of the image shared in the student case file
- [INFOGRAPHIC] Is This an Official Social Media Account?
- [PDF] Amazon Ad: Seeds for "Climbing Blue Strawberries"
- [ARTICLE] Are All Strawberries Red?

Process

1. Activating Prior Knowledge/Hook:

☑ Step/Tasks

a. Review the Four Lenses (see Chapters 1–4).
b. Review what students know about strawberries and how they are grown.
c. Review what students remember about a social media account's anatomy and how to investigate the account for clues.

⌾ Suggested Resources

For this step, check in the Digital Detective's Evidence Locker for links:

- [VIDEO] Clip depicting strawberry harvest in California
- [TEMPLATE] The Anatomy of a Social Media Account (a tool that may support students as they detect and document clues about a source's credibility)

2. Guided Practice Part 1: The Initial Hypothesis

☑ Step/Tasks

a. Working individually (or in pairs), have students review the one-sheet for The Case of . . . The Bodacious Blue Strawberries!
b. As they review the case, students should record and classify clues related to the Four Lenses.
   - ▶ Note: If you're using a traditional information literacy protocol (see Chapter 3) with students, now is the time to refer to it. However, remember that we recommend that these only be used as jumping-off points for learners: kindling to help spark their own investigations.
c. Product: By the end of this part of the lesson, student detective teams should generate an initial hypothesis or theory of the case.
d. Optional: Have students share their initial hypothesis with the group.

⌾ Suggested Resources

For this step, check in the Digital Detective's Evidence Locker for:

- [TEMPLATE] Evidence Log (a tool that may support students as they detect and document clues from the case)
- [TEMPLATE] Case Synopsis (a tool that may support students as they present their final verdicts in the case)

3. Guided Practice Part 2: The Case File

☑ Step/Tasks

a. Give students access to selected items from the case file.
b. Working in the same pairs and using the infographic Is This an Official Social Media Account (from the case file), students should consider what aspects of the account itself are potential credibility red flags.

🔘 Suggested Resources

For this step, check in the Digital Detective's Evidence Locker for:

- [INFOGRAPHIC] Is This an Official Social Media Account?

4. Assessment

✅ Step/Tasks

a. Individually, have students report their findings, including their final verdict regarding the story's credibility.

🔘 Suggested Resources

For this step, check in the Digital Detective's Evidence Locker for:

- [TEMPLATE] Case Synopsis

5. Whole Group Debrief

✅ Step/Tasks

a. Together, as a whole group, have students debate the various theories of the case.
b. Individually, or as a group, have students rate their own confidence in their verdict of the case.
   - ▶ We recommend using a Likert Scale for capturing this information. Digital tools such as Google Forms and Mentimeter are great options for creating this scale.

🔘 Suggested Resources

For this step, check in the Digital Detective's Evidence Locker for:

- [VIDEO] How to Use Likert Scales

6. Solution: Reveal the Facts of the Case! (See Below!)

✅ Step/Tasks

a. At this point, it's time to let students know where this story falls on the credibility spectrum. To do this, use the document The Facts of the Case (see the following section) to reveal the evidence associated with each lens that students should have uncovered.
b. We recommend that you also provide students with the opportunity to add evidence to the facts of the case. Students may have found other clues under each lens that can help their classmates think more deeply about credibility detection.

7. Synthesis

✓ Step/Tasks

To help students synthesize their learning, we want them to think more deeply about what kind of information makes them feel as though a source is credible and should be trusted.

a. Using a digital tool like Buncee, have students create their own social media profiles for an author, historical figure, or scientist. Challenge them to use as much credible information about the person as possible in creating the profile.
b. Then have students share their profile using a collaborative online space like Padlet.
c. Finally, have students review all profiles, indicating which they would follow by liking the post.

◉ Suggested Resources

For this step, check in the Digital Detective's Evidence Locker for links to:

- [VIDEO] Tutorial for Buncee
- [WEBSITE] "Fakebook" Profile Creator
- [VIDEO] Tutorial for Padlet

8. Reflection

✓ Step/Tasks

a. We recommend the "I used to think . . . but now I think . . . " reflection protocol, combined with a "think, pair, share" for this activity.
  ▶ First, individually, students compare what they used to believe about social media accounts before this activity with what they currently know to be right about judging their credibility.
  ▶ Then, in pairs, have students share and discuss their responses with a partner.

9. Scaffolds

Chapters 1 and 2 offer mini-lessons that may be helpful as scaffolds for this unit.

- Seek and Find: Community Reading Experience (Chapter 2, Access)
- Finish This Comic! 1 (Chapter 2, Access)
- Speed or Brake Activity (Chapter 1, Triggers)

10. Potential Extensions

- Using the picture book *I See, I See.* by Robert Henderson, have students consider how different people, from different backgrounds, with different perspectives, might view this story differently. Have students create a list of potential viewers of the story. Then, working in pairs, have them predict each potential viewer's likelihood to fall for the story of the bodacious blue strawberries, based on their unique perspectives.

THE FACTS OF THE CASE

Verdict **RED / FALSE** [Do Not Share]

Lens

LENS 1: TRIGGERS

Clues related to how elements of the story are designed to elicit, or trigger, an extreme emotional response.

Evidence

- While triggers are not the primary method of deception in this story, there are some elements that are worth noting as having the potential to trigger a strong emotional response:
  - ▶ The use of the ALL CAPS
  - ▶ The repeated chant of "USA!! USA!! USA!!" may trigger patriotism or other feelings toward Americans that could influence a person's perception of the information and/or their urge to trust or share the information.
- Asking learners to share what they think they know about the person who typed these words can help them understand how such elements trigger emotions that affect our work as Digital Detectives.

Lens

LENS 2: ACCESS

Clues related to the device upon which the story is being viewed and how that access might change the way a Digital Detective locates evidence.

Evidence

- Access plays a vital role in determining the credibility of this information and is the primary lens through which we should look at this case.
- Mobile devices add layers to the steps we may ask students to consider when parsing this story's accuracy.
  - ▶ Learners should consider the various steps required to locate information, such as the biographical information of the source.
- Additionally, because apps like Instagram add like/view counts to this story, learners should consider how those numbers influence their view of the information.

Lens

LENS 3: FORENSICS

Clues found in the details of the story, including (but not limited to) the URL, date published, authorship, and authority.

Evidence

- Considering whether or not this is an "official" account is also an integral part of determining whether the information is factual.
- Even though the account name includes the word *official*, clues like a lack of a profile photo should hint to students that the account may not be real.
  - ▸ Clicking the user ID gives us more information.
  - ▸ Additionally, since some sites offer badging to indicate whether an account has been verified, understanding what those markers are and how to find them can help learners identify valuable clues.

Lens

LENS 4: MOTIVES

Clues found in the motivations of potential suspects and how the story is created, shared, etc.

Evidence

- Although subtle, Motives is another critical lens for learners to consider as they evaluate this case.
  - ▸ Not only does the creator of this information masquerade as an official account sanctioned by the U.S. government, but they also make an attempt to spark competition between the U.S. and Japan. Ultimately, the creator of this information is hoping to influence our view of genetically modified produce by linking it to patriotism.
- **Lineup:** If you choose to do a lineup activity for this lesson, we suggest the following suspects: The Click Chaser, **The Mimicker**, The Troll, and The Wannabe. While The Mimicker is, ultimately, the correct answer, students will be able to make a compelling case for The Grifter as well. The distinction will be in The Grifter's goal of obtaining personal information, which is not present in this case.

The Case of . . . **The Greatest PIG of All Time?**

The Scene

This video of a baby pig saving a baby goat is going viral! By the time you see it on your friend Alex's feed, it's already gotten over 400,000 views!

The video features a baby goat struggling to swim in a pond, and the situation looks perilous! When it appears the goat might drown, a pink piglet swims to its rescue, helping its goat friend reach the shore just in the nick of time!

Alex loves it, so it must be true, right? Although Alex didn't record the video, his post includes a caption with his feelings about it, and the app has even featured his post.

Is this story real? And if not, is it Misinformation? Disinformation? Or Malinformation? What are Alex's intentions?

What do you notice from the screenshot alone that might provide you with some clues to this story's credibility?

Possible Clues (Questions to Think About)

- **Triggers:** How does this video make the viewer feel?
- **Access:** Does anything about how the information is presented in the app influence whether or not you think it's true?
- **Forensics:** How can we locate the original source of information?
- **Motives:** If this story turns out to be false or misleading, what kind of person would create/spread it?

Is this story about a pig turned superhero true, or is this just a bunch of nonsense?

💡 Big Ideas

This lesson focuses on the *Forensics* and *Triggers* Lenses. Although a lack of detail about the individuals who create and share information can be a credibility red flag, there's also value in understanding how knowing the source personally (or through online connections that can feel very personal) similarly affects our urge to trust or pass on information without proper vetting. These factors may also affect how we react to information emotionally. At the same time, we may recognize that an extreme emotional response to information is something to be wary of. When that information is shared by someone we trust, we are less likely to worry about the feelings that can cause us to let our guard down as Digital Detectives. The objectives below have been created to help learners interrogate the idea that while authorship and authority matter, so does proximity and relationship. Additionally, this lesson will help learners understand the difference between mis-, dis-, and malinformation.

🎺 SEL Spotlight

While we often caution learners to be on the lookout for information that triggers negative emotions, positive emotions that either make us feel good about ourselves or evoke feelings of love or admiration can also encourage us to lower our skepticism standards. Researchers have found that humans respond to baby animals' images positively because they trigger our urge to nurture or take care of them. Babies are non-threatening and require a great deal of attention, making them instantly trustworthy. Add to that a pumped-up cuddly factor, and we are all in (Bell, 2014). Neuroscientists aren't the only ones who recognize this—so do advertisers and the creators of false information. Negative feelings triggered by information are cause for suspicion. Still, they are overly positive if they trigger the urge to immediately share/pass on that information to others without further vetting. Additionally, suppose that information is shared by someone we know or trust. In that case, those positive feelings become connected to that relationship, which can weaken our resolve to vet what is being shared thoroughly. In this lesson, we challenge learners to consider the "awwww factor" in this story and how that may affect their work as Digital Detectives. Further, we challenge kids to think about how their proximity to those who create or posit the information they consume affects their urge to trust and share it. Through these activities, we encourage learners to:

- 🔍 Recognize how positive emotions can be used to manipulate behavior
- 🔍 Identify when relationships influence Digital Detective work
- 🔍 Become more aware of how those decisions affect their credibility

Curricula Connections

Target Audience	4th–5th (As with all lessons in this book, this grade span is a suggestion only. With a few adaptations, this lesson could easily apply to other learners.)

Potential Content Area Connections/Collaborations

- ELA: Prefixes and how they change words
- Science: The characteristics of baby animals that make us adore them and protect them from predators

ISTE Standards

Students

- Knowledge Constructor (3b): Students evaluate the accuracy, perspective, credibility and relevance of information, media, data or other resources.
- Knowledge Constructor (3d): Students build knowledge by actively exploring real-world issues and problems, developing ideas and theories and pursuing answers and solutions.
- Computational Thinker (5c): Students break problems into component parts, extract key information, and develop descriptive models to understand complex systems or facilitate problem-solving.

Educators

- Citizen (3b): Educators establish a learning culture that promotes curiosity and critical examination of online resources and fosters digital literacy and media fluency.
- Designer (5b): Educators design authentic learning activities that align with content area standards and use digital tools and resources to maximize active, deep learning.
- Facilitator (6b): Educators manage technology and student learning strategies in digital platforms, virtual environments, hands-on makerspaces or in the field.

Learning Objectives

By the end of this lesson:

- The learner will apply the Four Lenses to information as a step in determining credibility.
- The learner will understand the difference between misinformation, disinformation, and malinformation.
- The learner will understand how their relationship and proximity to an information source can affect their urge to trust and share that information.
- The learner will examine how positive emotions can be used as triggers to spread false information.
- The learner will develop and share a hypothesis related to information credibility.
- The learner will synthesize learning by identifying which type of false information is present in the story and then using evidence from the case to explain and justify this conclusion.
- The learner will synthesize learning by brainstorming examples of each type of false information.

Resources Needed for This Lesson

Reminder: A variety of resources related to this chapter can be found in the Digital Detective's Evidence Locker. Use the QR code to the left or visit evidencelocker.online. Then navigate to Chapter 8.

Time Needed for This Lesson: 2–4 hours

Case File

The following supplemental resources from the Digital Detective's Evidence Locker may be given to students to examine the case:

- [IMAGE] Hi-res version of the image shared in the student case file
- [VIDEO] Pig Saves Baby Goat
- [VIDEO] The House Hippo
- [VIDEO] Fake News Explained (from the CBC)
- [INFOGRAPHIC] Seeing Is Believing. Or Is It?
- [INFOGRAPHIC] Spot the Difference
- [INFOGRAPHIC] Feast or Famine

Process

1. Activating Prior Knowledge/Hook:

☑ Step/Tasks

a. Review the Four Lenses (see Chapters 1–4).
b. Review what students know about petting zoos.
c. Have students brainstorm the words/phrases that they most often associate with baby animals.
d. Review what students know about video-specific social media (like Snapchat or TikTok). Have they ever seen an altered video on these sites?

◉ Suggested Resources

For this step, check in the Digital Detective's Evidence Locker for links to:

- [VIDEO] Virtual Tour of Zoo Atlanta's Petting Zoo
- [INFOGRAPHIC] Seeing Is Believing. Or Is It?

2. Guided Practice Part 1: The Initial Hypothesis

☑ Step/Tasks

a. Working individually (or in pairs), have students review the one-sheet for The Case of . . . The Greatest PIG of All Time?
b. Students should record and classify clues related to the Four Lenses as they review the case.
  ► Note: If you're using a traditional information literacy protocol (see Chapter 3) with students, now is the time to refer to it. However, remember that we recommend that these only be used as jumping-off points for learners: kindling to help spark their own investigations.
c. Product: By the end of this part of the lesson, student detective teams should generate an initial hypothesis or theory of the case.
d. Optional: Have students share their initial hypothesis with the whole group.

◉ Suggested Resources

For this step, check in the Digital Detective's Evidence Locker for links to:

- [TEMPLATE] Evidence Log (a tool that may support students as they detect and document clues from the case)
- [TEMPLATE] Case Synopsis (a tool that may support students as they present their final verdicts in the case)

3. Guided Practice Part 2: The Case File

☑ Step/Tasks

1. Give students access to selected items from the case file, noting that some of these items reveal the facts of the case.
2. Working in the same pairs and using the infographic Does This Pass the WHOA! Test?, have students identify clues that this story might be too good (or, in this case, too cute!) to be true.
3. Then, working in the same pairs and using the infographic Feast or Famine and a tool like Popplet, have students process the case file as though the source of information hasn't been shared by "Alex" but, instead, by someone they trust: This could be their teacher, a relative, or another classmate.
   ▶ Does this change their hypothesis?

🔘 Suggested Resources

For this step, check in the Digital Detective's Evidence Locker for links to:

- [INFOGRAPHIC] Does This Pass the WHOA! Test?
- [TEMPLATE] Does This Pass the WHOA! Test?
- [INFOGRAPHIC] Feast or Famine
- [INFOGRAPHIC] What Happens When You Know the Secondary Source?
- [VIDEO] Tutorial for Popplet

4. Assessment

☑ Step/Tasks

At this point, students should be ready to deliver a verdict on the case.

a. Individually, have students report their findings, including their final verdict regarding the story's credibility. You may think of recording student responses using the Case Synopsis template from the Digital Detective's Notebook or a digital voting tool, such as Kahoot!, Poll Everywhere, or Socrative.

🔘 Suggested Resources

For this step, check in the Digital Detective's Evidence Locker for:

- [TEMPLATE] Case Synopsis

5. Whole Group Debrief

☑ Step/Tasks

a. Together, as a whole group, have students debate the various theories of the case.
b. Individually, or as a group, have students rate their confidence in their verdict of the case.
   ► We recommend using a Likert Scale for capturing this information. Digital tools such as Google Forms and Mentimeter are great options for creating this scale.

◉ Suggested Resources

For this step, check in the Digital Detective's Evidence Locker for links to:

- [VIDEO] How to Use Likert Scales

6. Solution: Reveal the Facts of the Case! (See Below!)

☑ Step/Tasks

a. At this point, it's time to let students know where this story fell on the credibility spectrum. To do this, use the document The Facts of the Case (see the following section) to reveal the evidence associated with each lens that students should have uncovered.
b. We recommend that you also provide students with the opportunity to add evidence to the case's facts. Students may have found other clues under each lens to help their classmates think more deeply about credibility detection.

7. Synthesis

☑ Step/Tasks

To help students synthesize their learning, we want them to think more deeply about what type of false information was present in this case.

a. Using the Spot the Difference infographic from the Evidence Locker, have students consider whether this information was an example of misinformation, disinformation, or malinformation.
b. Citing specific details from the case, have students identify which form of false information this story represents.
c. Using a digital tool like Buncee, have students complete a graphic organizer to brainstorm examples of each type of false information.
d. Finally, have students think about how they might use what they've learned to have a conversation with "Alex" (or the person they considered a potential trustworthy source earlier) to help that person understand how this story was false, as well as the difference between mis-, dis-, and malinformation.

◉ Suggested Resources

For this step, check in the Digital Detective's Evidence Locker for links to:

- [INFOGRAPHIC] Spot the Difference
- [GRAPHIC ORGANIZER] Buncee
- [VIDEO] Tutorial for Buncee

8. Reflection

☑ Step/Tasks

a. We recommend the Dinner Table reflection strategy for this exercise. Working in small groups, have students share what they would tell their families about this exercise when asked, "What did you do in school today?"

9. Scaffolds

- Chapters 1 and 3 offer mini-lessons that may be helpful as scaffolds for this unit.
  - ▶ Information Literacy Likert Scale/Mood Meter (Chapter 1, Triggers)
  - ▶ Speed or Brake Activity (Chapter 1, Triggers)
  - ▶ Finish This Comic! 1 (Chapter 3, Forensics)

10. Potential Extensions

- Using pages 32–33 of the book *Trending: How and Why Stuff Gets Popular* by Kira Vermond, have students make a list of ways the baby pig saving the baby goat is similar to the story of Unicorn Frappuccinos. (Note: Did your students notice any similarities in the way these two stories were created?)
- Depending on the level of your students, you might think about teaching storyboarding. Have the students rewrite the story of the "greatest PIG of all time" without using deception. Consider asking questions:

  a. What makes someone or something great?
  b. What is a hero? How does one become a hero in their community?

- Note: Although a bit complex for elementary students, teaching simple elements of the hero's journey can be applied within the context of this lesson. Several age-appropriate books and clips from Disney movies can serve as simple examples to help with a more complex understanding in later grades.

THE FACTS OF THE CASE

Verdict **YELLOW / FALSE** (but not harmful)
[Share Only with Explanation]

Lens

LENS 1: TRIGGERS

Clues related to how elements of the story are designed to elicit, or trigger, an extreme emotional response.

Evidence

- Triggers are an essential method of deception in this story. Here are some triggers students may pick up on:
  - ▶ The use of "cute" baby animals may have contributed to their urge to trust/share this story.
  - ▶ The alarmed voice used to narrate the video.
  - ▶ The use of the term *hero* to describe the pig.
  - ▶ The use of the phrase *simply amazing* in the description.
- By applying the WHOA! Test, students should reflect on how the original video was designed to go viral.

Lens

LENS 2: ACCESS

Clues related to the device upon which the story is being viewed and how that access might change the way a Digital Detective locates evidence.

Evidence

- Access plays a role in our response to this story. The app used in the one-sheet classroom resource (in this case, TikTok) includes personalization options to cater to engagement:
  - ▶ Likes
  - ▶ Share counts
  - ▶ Music choice to go along with the post
- Also, it draws out the story with the adjective *featured* to exhibit a vetted feel.
- These personalization elements and the Community Reading Experience may play a role in our urge to trust/share this story.

LENS 3: FORENSICS

Clues found in the details of the story, including (but not limited to) the URL, date published, authorship, and authority.

Evidence

- Ultimately, this is an example of disinformation, specifically a hoax. Some clues students should pick up on are:
  - ▶ By clicking on the profile of the person who posted the video, students will find a suspicious lack of information about the source.
  - ▶ This video is the only media the person had posted (as of this writing).
  - ▶ The person talking in the video is not identified.
- Suppose you have students use an information literacy protocol as part of this work. In that case, they should examine each component of that protocol related to this case. Doing so may lead to other clues.
- Considering whether this is an example of misinformation, disinformation, or malinformation will help learners identify other potential credibility red flags.

LENS 4: MOTIVES

Clues found in the motivations of potential suspects and how the story is created, shared, etc.

Evidence

- This case provides an exciting opportunity to discuss the motives of individuals who create misleading information for reasons other than to cause harm.
- Ultimately, this was a hoax created to generate excitement for a TV show and, hopefully, increase viewership.
- **Lineup:** If you choose to do a lineup activity for this lesson, we suggest the following suspects: The Jokester, **The Influencer for Hire**, The Troll, and The Flash Bomber. While The Influencer for Hire is, ultimately, the correct answer, students will be able to make a compelling case for The Jokester as well. The distinction will be in The Influencer for Hire's desire to make money.

The Case of . . . **Chew On This!**

The Scene

A trip to the dentist is bad enough when your mouth contains only the typical 32 teeth. Imagine going when you have over 500!

This story features a boy in India whose mouth was crowded with 526 teeth. His parents took the 7-year-old to the doctor when he complained of jaw pain, never suspecting that he would need nearly five hours of surgery to remove a record-breaking number of teeth.

Adding to the problem is a lack of dental care in the area of India where this boy lives. Had he been to the dentist earlier, the problem might have been fixed sooner.

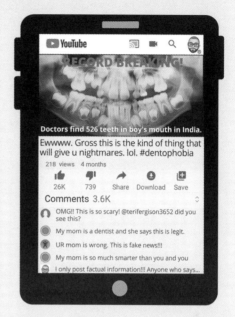

This story continues to be shared because it is shocking and disturbing, but is it true?

Possible Clues (Questions to Think About)

- **Triggers:** How does this information make you feel? Do these emotions affect your urge to trust or share the information?
- **Access:** Does the presence of comments and/or like and share counts affect your ability to determine fact from fiction?
- **Forensics:** How can we locate the original source of the information?
- **Motives:** If this story turns out to be false or misleading, what kind of person would create/spread it?

Is this story about dental drama true, or did we just sink our teeth into some dental deceit?

💡 Big Ideas

This lesson focuses on the *Triggers* and *Forensics* Lenses. There are many ways that emotions can hijack the process of determining fact from fiction in the information we consume. While we often caution readers to consider the triggering of negative emotions as a strategy for making us trust false information, those same emotions can also stand between us and information that is true or even important. If a story, post, or video makes us feel extremely upset or fearful, that's a signal for us to press pause and manage those emotions before moving forward. However, it doesn't always mean the information is false. Moreover, some elements of the Community Reading Experience can add fuel to the emotional fire. Emotions that have been triggered by the information itself can be intensified by the presence of likes, view counts, and user comments. The objectives below were created to help learners manage those emotions to move onto the crucial step of uncovering forensic clues to the information's credibility. This lesson will also help learners understand the difference between a primary and a secondary source in the digital age.

📣 SEL Spotlight

One of the reasons traditional approaches to news literacy fail to be applied outside of school is that our students haven't yet learned how to manage the emotional triggers embedded throughout their screen-filled lives. Even when the information is factual, emotional triggers remain an influential factor as we make quick decisions about trusting and sharing information. In this lesson, we challenge learners to:

- Recognize when emotional triggers influence decisions made as Digital Detectives
- Understand how the Community Reading Experience provides additional access points for emotional triggers
- Consider their responsibility when sharing information that contains emotion-baiting content

Curricula Connections

Target Audience	4th–5th (As with all lessons in this book, this grade span is a suggestion only. With a few adaptations, this lesson could easily be applied to other learners.)

Potential Content Area Connections/Collaborations

- Science: Human anatomy, including the probability of growing superfluous teeth and how extra teeth affect other body functions
- Social Studies: Healthcare in India, the evolution of primary versus secondary sources
- Career-Related Learning (CTE): How X-ray/MRI devices help professionals in some careers do their jobs more effectively (see Potential Extensions)

ISTE Standards

Students

- Knowledge Constructor (3b): Students evaluate the accuracy, perspective, credibility and relevance of information, media, data or other resources.
- Knowledge Constructor (3d): Students build knowledge by actively exploring real-world issues and problems, developing ideas and theories and pursuing answers and solutions.
- Computational Thinker (5c): Students break problems into component parts, extract key information, and develop descriptive models to understand complex systems or facilitate problem-solving.

Educators

- Citizen (3b): Educators establish a learning culture that promotes curiosity and critical examination of online resources and fosters digital literacy and media fluency.
- Designer (5b): Educators design authentic learning activities that align with content area standards and use digital tools and resources to maximize active, deep learning.
- Facilitator (6b): Educators manage the use of technology and student learning strategies in digital platforms, virtual environments, hands-on makerspaces or in the field.
- Analyst (7b): Educators use technology to design and implement a variety of formative and summative assessments that accommodate learner needs, provide timely feedback to students and inform instruction.

Learning Objectives

By the end of this lesson:

- The learner will apply the Four Lenses to information as a step in determining credibility.
- The learner will identify ways that emotional triggers influence Digital Detective work.
- The learner will analyze how the Community Reading Experience contributes to the potency of emotional triggers in the information we consume.
- The learner will develop and share a hypothesis related to information credibility.
- The learner will synthesize learning by creating a PSA to help other learners recognize and manage the emotions triggered by the information we consume.

Resources Needed for This Lesson

Reminder: A variety of resources related to this chapter can be found in the Digital Detective's Evidence Locker. Use the QR code to the left, or visit evidencelocker.online. Then navigate to Chapter 8.

Time Needed for This Lesson: 2–4 hours

Case File

The following supplemental resources from the Digital Detective's Evidence Locker may be given to students to help them examine the case. Be sure to note which resources for this story reveal the facts of the case.

- [IMAGE] Hi-res version of the image shared in the student case file
- [VIDEO] Doctors Remove 526 Teeth from Boy's Mouth
- [ARTICLE] Guinness Book of World Records: Teeth
- [ARTICLE] My Son Has Shark Teeth
- [RESOURCE COLLECTION] Fear of Dentists Memes
- [INFOGRAPHIC] Digital Age Primary vs. Secondary Sources
- [INFOGRAPHIC] Is This an Official Social Media Account?

Process

1. Activating Prior Knowledge/Hook:

☑ Step/Tasks

a. Review the Four Lenses (see Chapters 1–4).
b. Have students share their experiences of going to the dentist.
c. Have students share what they know about India.

🌀 Suggested Resources

For this step, check in the Digital Detective's Evidence Locker for:

- [VIDEO] Clip of a virtual tour of what it's like to go to school in India

2. Guided Practice Part 1: The Initial Hypothesis

☑ Step/Tasks

a. Working individually (or in pairs), have students review the one-sheet for The Case of . . . Chew On This!
b. As they review the case, students should record and classify clues related to the Four Lenses.
   - ▶ Note: If you're using a traditional information literacy protocol (see Chapter 3) with students, now is the time to refer to it. However, remember that we recommend that these only be used as jumping-off points for learners: kindling to help spark their own investigations.
c. Product: By the end of this part of the lesson, student detective teams should generate an initial hypothesis or theory of the case.
d. Optional: Have students share their initial hypothesis with the group.

🌀 Suggested Resources

For this step, check in the Digital Detective's Evidence Locker for:

- [TEMPLATE] Evidence Log (a tool that may support students as they detect and document clues from the case)
- [TEMPLATE] Case Synopsis (a tool that may support students as they present their final verdicts in the case)

3. Guided Practice Part 2: The Case File

☑ Step/Tasks

a. Give students access to selected items from the case file, noting that some of these items reveal the facts of the case.
b. Working in the same pairs, and using the infographic Digital Age Primary vs. Secondary Sources, have students see if they can trace this story back to its original source.
   - ▶ This may also be a good time to review what students know about "official" or verified social media accounts.

🌀 Suggested Resources

For this step, check in the Digital Detective's Evidence Locker for links to:

- [INFOGRAPHIC] Digital Age Primary vs. Secondary Sources
- [TEMPLATE] Dusting for Digital Footprints

4. Assessment

☑ Step/Tasks

At this point, students should be ready to deliver a verdict on the case.

a. Individually, have students report their findings, including their final verdict regarding the story's credibility. Student responses can be recorded using the Case Synopsis template from the Digital Detective's Notebook or through a digital voting tool, such as Kahoot!, Poll Everywhere, or Socrative.

◉ Suggested Resources

For this step, check in the Digital Detective's Evidence Locker for:

- [TEMPLATE] Case Synopsis

5. Whole Group Debrief

☑ Step/Tasks

a. Together, as a whole group, have students debate the various theories of the case.
b. Individually, or as a group, have students rate their own confidence in their verdict of the case.
   ► We recommend using a Likert Scale for capturing this information. Digital tools such as Google Forms and Mentimeter are great options for creating this scale.

◉ Suggested Resources

For this step, check in the Digital Detective's Evidence Locker for:

- [VIDEO] How to Use Likert Scales

6. Solution: Reveal the Facts of the Case! (See Below!)

☑ Step/Tasks

a. At this point, it's time to let students know where this story fell on the credibility spectrum. To do this, use the document The Facts of the Case (see the following section) to reveal the evidence associated with each lens that students should have uncovered.
b. We recommend that you also provide students with the opportunity to add evidence to the facts of the case. Students may have found other clues under each lens that can help their classmates think more deeply about credibility detection.

7. Synthesis

☑ Step/Tasks

To help students synthesize their learning, we want them to think more deeply about both pressing pause when emotions trigger them and what their role is as a member of an online community whose likes, shares, and comments might influence others.

a. Individually, using the infographic Knowing When and How to Press Pause and the resource collection More Ways to Press Pause, have students identify the three emotions that are most likely to be triggered by this story and most likely to influence whether someone trusts or shares it.

b. Then, working in pairs, and using the infographics What's Not to Like? and Knowing When and How to Press Pause, students should consider what parts of the story itself as well as aspects of the Community Reading Experience might influence their work as Digital Detectives. Their findings may be recorded using the Social Media Mood Chart from the Digital Detective's Notebook in the Evidence Locker.
   ▶ Optional: This may be a good time to walk students through a few ways to press pause when they find themselves being triggered by information. The resource collection Ways to Press Pause may be useful for this work.

c. Then, working in small groups, and using a digital poster-making tool (like Buncee), have students create digital posters sharing tips for being productive members of online information communities. Now that they understand how elements such as likes, shares, and comments can trigger emotional responses and influence others, their poster should reflect the ways they intend to use those tools to stop the spread of false information.

◉ Suggested Resources

For this step, check in the Digital Detective's Evidence Locker for links to:

- [INFOGRAPHIC] What's Not to Like?
- [INFOGRAPHIC] Knowing When and How to Press Pause
- [TEMPLATE] Social Media Mood Chart
- [RESOURCE COLLECTION] More Ways to Press Pause

8. Reflection

☑ Step/Tasks

We recommend the SAP reflection protocol for this activity.

a. Start by asking learners to describe sap from a tree. (Anchor the discussion toward sap being sticky.)

b. Then share the idea that learning is best when it is "sticky" because then it's not easily forgotten.

c. For their reflection, have students share the following ways today's lesson has been sticky:
   S: Something I learned is . . .
   (An important takeaway from the lesson.)
   A: A question I still have is . . .
   (Something that is still confusing.)
   P: Please help me plan . . .
   (Steps they will take as a result of this learning.)

9. Scaffolds

Chapters 1 and 3 offer mini-lessons that may be helpful as scaffolds for this unit.

- Information Literacy Likert Scale/Mood Meter (Chapter 1, Triggers)
- Speed or Brake Activity (Chapter 1, Triggers)
- Finish This Comic! 1 (Chapter 3, Forensics)

10. Potential Extensions

- In the graphic novel *Smile*, Raina Telgemeier shares the true story of how she lost her two front teeth after falling while getting off the bus. The damage to her teeth lasts several years, multiple sets of braces, and lots of tears. After showing the book trailer for this graphic novel, have students create a social media post about Raina's fall and subsequent dental drama. Have them imagine who would post it, who would comment, and how Raina might react to the post herself. Would knowing the poster influence how others view it?

THE FACTS OF THE CASE

Verdict **GREEN** | **TRUE** [Share with Credit]

Lens

LENS 1: TRIGGERS

Clues related to how elements of the story are designed to elicit, or trigger, an extreme emotional response.

Evidence

- Even though this story is true, triggers are an important element to consider when evaluating the information. Triggers don't just cause us to believe false information. They may also cause us to dismiss true information. Here are some triggers students may pick up on:
  - ▶ The graphic nature of the image
  - ▶ Existing biases and fears related to going to the dentist

Lens

LENS 2: ACCESS

Clues related to the device upon which the story is being viewed and how that access might change the way a Digital Detective locates evidence.

Evidence

- Access plays a role in our response to this story. Apps like YouTube not only feature like and share counts but also automatically sort comments by most popular. Students should be aware of how this peripheral information influences their work as Digital Detectives. For example, comments that reflect their own fears related to going to the dentist may feel validating or justify the urge to dismiss this story as being too scary to be true.
- Additionally, unless a secondary source reveals where the video originally came from, YouTube doesn't provide a pathway to this information. Digital Detectives must dig deeper. (In this case, students have accessed this video through a secondary source.)

LENS 3: FORENSICS

Clues found in the details of the story, including (but not limited to) the URL, date published, authorship, and authority.

Evidence

- The Forensics Lens is critical for this story. Some clues students should pick up on are:
  - ▶ Students may recognize CBS as a mainstream news channel. (Clicking the user profile reveals more information.)
  - ▶ The video contains live footage from the event with eyewitness accounts.
  - ▶ The video contains details—such as names, locations, and dates—that can be verified.

LENS 4: MOTIVES

Clues found in the motivations of potential suspects and how the story is created, shared, etc.

Evidence

- The original source of this information was a press release issued by the hospital that performed the surgery. Their goal was to educate people in their region about oral health.
- The "suspect" in this case is The Teacher and their motives still matter. What might motivate the doctors who made this video to share the story rather than just keeping it private? Similarly, what might motivate the parents to allow this video of their child to be shared worldwide?
- **Lineup:** If you choose to do a lineup activity for this lesson, we suggest the following suspects: The Jokester, The Blue Liar, The Click Chaser, and The Lemming. Because this story is true, the correct answer will be **None of the Above**. However, students may make compelling arguments for any of these suspects.

The Case of . . . **The 450lb Dog!**

The Scene

Imagine learning that your furry best friend has a rare medical disorder that will cause their bones to grow to epic proportions. That's exactly what happened when Christopher Cline took his dog Juji to the vet to find out why he hadn't stopped growing.

Although the vet assured Chris that this rare disorder wouldn't cause Juji pain, it would come with a unique set of challenges, including how to find a collar that fits and where to store all that dog food.

Over three million people have viewed Chris and Juji's story, but is it real? Is Juji really the world's largest dog, or is this just an example of a gigantic lie?

What do you notice from the screenshot alone that might provide you with some clues to this story's credibility?

Possible Clues (Questions to Think About)

- **Triggers:** How does this information make you feel? Does anything about it make you hope that it's true or that it isn't?
- **Access:** Does the app being used make it easier or more difficult to locate clues?
- **Forensics:** What do you notice about the profile/account that shared this story?
- **Motives:** If this story turns out to be fake, what might motivate someone to create/share it?

Is this story about a mammoth mutt true, or has its credibility gone to the dogs?

💡 Big Ideas

This lesson focuses on the *Motives* and *Forensics* Lenses. In Chapter 4, we unpacked the various motives of potential "suspects" who may be responsible for creating suspicious content. In this chapter, we want to dig a little deeper into the financial incentives that drive a lot of this activity. For some of our students, the internet is ubiquitous. Even though they may not have access to broadband at home, we know that the majority of American families have access to the internet through smartphones. Additionally, access to free internet is commonplace at public libraries and even many fast food restaurants. However, we know that as Andrew Lewis famously said, "If you're not paying for it, you're not the customer; you're the product being sold" (2010). The objectives below were designed to help learners better understand the relationship between clicks and cash.

📢 SEL Spotlight

As we mentioned in Chapter 1, to most educators, the word *firewall* calls to mind a computer system designed to block unauthorized access and protect users from unsafe content. But for decades, the news and media had their own philosophical version of a firewall: the tradition of separating news content from the business of raising revenue through advertising. This prevented the need to make money from influencing how the news is reported. In recent years, this separation has all but disappeared as more and more people become unwilling to pay for information. In a world where very few people subscribe to news and expect information to be free, those responsible for creating and hosting content have had to find new ways to make money: enter click-driven advertisements. In this model, the more we click, the more money the advertiser, hosting service, and, ultimately, content creator make. The trick is getting us to click. One incredibly effective strategy for increasing engagement with online content is to embed emotional triggers at every access point. In this lesson, we challenge students to think about the strategies someone might employ to increase the likelihood that we will click on a story. Through these activities, we encourage learners to:

- Recognize when they are the product being sold
- Understand how an emotional response to information increases the likelihood that they will engage with advertorial content

Curricula Connections

Target Audience	4th–5th (As with all lessons in this book, this grade span is a suggestion only. With a few adaptations, this lesson could easily be applied to other learners.)

Potential Content Area Connections/Collaborations

- Science: Bone disorders, gigantism
- Math: Scale factor, percentages, number sense

ISTE Standards

Students

- Knowledge Constructor (3b): Students evaluate the accuracy, perspective, credibility and relevance of information, media, data or other resources.
- Knowledge Constructor (3d): Students build knowledge by actively exploring real-world issues and problems, developing ideas and theories and pursuing answers and solutions.
- Computational Thinker (5c): Students break problems into component parts, extract key information, and develop descriptive models to understand complex systems or facilitate problem-solving.

Educators

- Citizen (3b): Educators establish a learning culture that promotes curiosity and critical examination of online resources and fosters digital literacy and media fluency.
- Designer (5b): Educators design authentic learning activities that align with content area standards and use digital tools and resources to maximize active, deep learning.
- Facilitator (6b): Educators manage the use of technology and student learning strategies in digital platforms, virtual environments, hands-on makerspaces or in the field.

Learning Objectives

By the end of this lesson:

- The learner will apply the Four Lenses to information as a step in determining credibility.
- The learner will understand how consumer clicks generate money for advertisers.
- The learner will identify content that has been created to increase user engagement (clicks).
- The learner will develop and share a hypothesis related to information credibility.
- The learner will synthesize learning by estimating how much money could have been made from this story (given a specific formula).
- The learner will synthesize learning through role-play, by acting out a conversation explaining how money is made through online advertising to another person.

Resources Needed for This Lesson

Reminder: A variety of resources related to this chapter can be found in the Digital Detective's Evidence Locker. Use the QR code to the left, or visit evidencelocker.online. Then navigate to Chapter 8.

Time Needed for This Lesson: 2–4 hours

Case File

The following supplemental resources from Digital Detective's Evidence Locker may be given to students to help them examine the case. Be sure to note which resources for this story reveal the facts of the case.

- [IMAGE] Hi-res version of image shared in student case file
- [VIDEO] This Dog Is 450lbs (from Instagram)
- [LINKS] Links to related Instagram profiles
- [INFOGRAPHIC] Follow the Money
- [TEMPLATE] Dusting for Prints | Motives

Process

1. Activating Prior Knowledge/Hook:

☑ Step/Tasks

a. Review the Four Lenses (see Chapters 1–4).
b. Take a poll to discover how many students have pets. You may even want to sort that list into types (cats, dogs, etc.).
c. Because this lesson involves a video from the website The Dodo, have students explore the site's Odd Couples playlist. See if they can identify the purpose of the site/channel (which is to post adorable animal content).

◉ Suggested Resources

For this step, check in the Digital Detective's Evidence Locker for a link to:

- [VIDEO] Odd Couples Playlist from The Dodo

2. Guided Practice Part 1: The Initial Hypothesis

☑ Step/Tasks

a. Working individually (or in pairs), have students review the one-sheet for The Case of . . . The 450lb Dog!!
b. As they review the case, students should record and classify clues related to the Four Lenses.
   ▶ Note: If you're using a traditional information literacy protocol (see Chapter 3) with students, now is the time to refer to it. However, remember that we recommend that these only be used as jumping-off points for learners: kindling to help spark their own investigations.
c. Product: By the end of this part of the lesson, student detective teams should generate an initial hypothesis or theory of the case.
d. Optional: Have students share their initial hypothesis with the group.

◉ Suggested Resources

For this step, check in the Digital Detective's Evidence Locker for:

- [TEMPLATE] Evidence Log (a tool that may support students as they detect and document clues from the case)
- [TEMPLATE] Case Synopsis (a tool that may support students as they present their final verdicts in the case)

3. Guided Practice Part 2: The Case File

☑ Step/Tasks

a. Give students access to selected items from the case file, noting that some of these items reveal the facts of the case.
b. Working in the same pairs and using the infographic Follow the Money, students should think about how this information applies to the story of the 450lb dog.
c. Student responses can be recorded using the Dusting for Prints | Motives template from the Digital Detective's Notebook.

◉ Suggested Resources

For this step, check in the Digital Detective's Evidence Locker for:

- [INFOGRAPHIC] Follow the Money
- [TEMPLATE] Dusting for Prints | Motives

4. Assessment

☑ Step/Tasks

At this point, students should be ready to deliver a verdict on the case.

a. Individually, have students report their findings, including their final verdict regarding the story's credibility. Student responses can be recorded using the Case Synopsis template from the Digital Detective's Notebook or through a digital voting tool, such as Kahoot!, Poll Everywhere, or Socrative.

◉ Suggested Resources

For this step, check in the Digital Detective's Evidence Locker for:

- [TEMPLATE] Case Synopsis

5. Whole Group Debrief

☑ Step/Tasks

a. Together, as a whole group, have students debate the various theories of the case.
b. Individually, or as a group, have students rate their own confidence in their verdict of the case.
  ▶ We recommend using a Likert Scale for capturing this information. Digital tools such as Google Forms and Mentimeter are great options for creating this scale.

◉ Suggested Resources

For this step, check in the Digital Detective's Evidence Locker for:

  ▶ [VIDEO] How to Use Likert Scales

6. Solution: Reveal the Facts of the Case! (See Below!)

a. At this point, it's time to let students know where this story fell on the credibility spectrum. To do this, use the document The Facts of the Case (see the following section) to reveal the evidence associated with each lens that students should have uncovered.
b. We recommend that you also provide students with the opportunity to add evidence to the facts of the case. Students may have found other clues under each lens that can help their classmates think more deeply about credibility detection.

7. Synthesis

☑ Step/Tasks

To help students synthesize their learning, we want them to think more deeply about secondary sources.

a. Using the Genially game Big Money and the 450lb Dog, students can calculate the amount of money that could potentially be made through the content in this story.
b. Using a blank comic strip template (such as the In Your Own Words template, found in the Evidence Locker), have students role play a conversation in which they explain to another person how much money can be made using a story like the 450lb dog.

◉ Suggested Resources

For this step, check in the Digital Detective's Evidence Locker for links to:

- [GAME] Big Money and the 450lb Dog on Genially
- [TEMPLATE] In Your Own Words comic strip

8. Reflection

☑ Step/Tasks

a. We recommend the WOOF! reflection protocol for this activity. In pairs, or using a digital tool like Flipgrid, have students respond to the following prompts:
  ▶ **W**ho will you tell about this lesson later today?
  ▶ **O**ne new thing you learned today
  ▶ **O**ne question you still have
  ▶ **F**rom now on, when online, what's one thing you'll do differently?

9. Scaffolds

Chapters 3 and 4 offer mini-lessons that may be helpful as scaffolds for this unit.

- Writing Good Questions (Chapter 3, Forensics)
- Finish This Comic! 1 (Chapter 3, Forensics)
- Heads Up Game, Version 1 (Chapter 4, Motives)

10. Potential Extensions

Using the book *The Dodo: 50 Odd Couples*, have students select an incredible story that they feel could be turned into a viral video. Then have them share a marketing plan to increase the video's income potential. Have them create and share a headline and description that would be sure to get people to click. Then have them imagine what types of products would make sense as potential advertisements within the video.

Verdict **YELLOW | FALSE** (but Not Harmful) [Share Only with Explanation]

Lens

LENS 1: TRIGGERS

Clues related to how elements of the story are designed to elicit, or trigger, an extreme emotional response.

Evidence

- Triggers play an important role in this case because their purpose is to generate more clicks. Some clues that students may recognize as attempts to trigger emotions might include:
  - ▶ Thumbnail of giant dog (might trigger shock/disbelief or a feeling of trust toward the cute dog)
  - ▶ The emojis used in the description (might trigger emotions such as shock)

Lens

LENS 2: ACCESS

Clues related to the device upon which the story is being viewed and how that access might change the way a Digital Detective locates evidence.

Evidence

- Access plays a role in our response to this story. Apps like Instagram feature a Community Reading Experience that include like/share counts that may influence us.
- Mobile devices also provide us with instant share features, making it very easy for us to share without digging deeper to make sure a story is accurate.

Lens

LENS 3: FORENSICS

Clues found in the details of the story, including (but not limited to) the URL, date published, authorship, and authority.

Evidence

- The Forensics Lens is critical for this story. Some clues students should pick up on are:
  - ▶ While The Dodo is a legitimate source of factual information, the creator of the video is tagged in their post. Clicking the user profile gives students more information.
  - ▶ The video was posted on April Fool's Day.
  - ▶ While the content appears as a video, there is no video footage of the dog; only still images are included.

Lens

LENS 4: MOTIVES

Clues found in the motivations of potential suspects and how the story is created, shared, etc.

Evidence

- The Motives Lens is critical for this story. Some clues students should pick up on are:
  - ▶ The biographical information of the photographer who created the images includes the disclaimer that he produces these images for money.
  - ▶ The date is a huge clue as to motivation as well. In the end, this was a viral April Fool's Day hoax.
- **Lineup:** If you choose to do a lineup activity for this lesson, we suggest the following suspects: **The Jokester**, The Influencer for Hire, The Wannabe, and The Lemming. While The Joker is, ultimately, the correct answer, students will be able to make a compelling case for The Influencer for Hire, the distinction being that no one hired this suspect to create the content.

Digital Detective's Lessons for Middle Grade Learners

This chapter consists of four lessons designed to help middle grade learners assume the role of Digital Detective by applying the Four Lenses to a broad array of news stories from various information sources.

These lessons are supported by tools and resources to help you implement them as soon as you feel your Digital Detectives are ready to start cracking cases. As noted earlier, we encourage you to think outside the grade spans we've identified. For example, if you teach middle grade learners, we hope you'll explore the cases designed for both elementary and high school learners, too. With your experience brought to bear, we're betting some of those lessons could be reworked for your Digital Detectives as well.

Contents

The Case of . . . **The 911 Toilet Paper Emergency!**

The Scene

One unexpected consequence of the COVID-19 global health crisis was a nation-wide shortage of toilet paper. As people prepared for a possibly lengthy quarantine, stocking up on bathroom tissue proved impossible in many locations.

Police in Newport, Oregon, used social media to plead with the public to stop calling 911 to report being out of toilet paper. A Facebook post by the Newport Police Department urged residents to stay calm and not panic if they run out of toilet paper.

The initial Facebook post was seen and shared by numerous news outlets including CNN, Fox News, and NPR.

Possible Clues (Questions to Think About)

- **Triggers:** How does this information make you feel about the people involved—the police and those calling 911?
- **Access:** Does the presence of comments and/or like and share counts affect your ability to determine fact from fiction?
- **Forensics:** When was this story posted? Does the timing in any way influence its credibility?
- **Motives:** If this story turns out to be false or misleading, what kind of person would create/spread it?

Were people REALLY calling 911 for TP, or does this story not smell right?

💡 Big Ideas

This lesson focuses on the *Triggers* and *Forensics* Lenses. There are many ways that emotions can hijack the process of determining fact from fiction in the information we consume. While we often caution readers to consider the triggering of negative emotions as a strategy for making us trust false information, those same emotions can also stand between us and information that is true or even important. If a story, post, or video makes us feel extremely upset or fearful, that's a signal for us to press pause and manage those emotions before moving forward. However, it doesn't always mean the information is false. Moreover, some elements of the Community Reading Experience can add fuel to the emotional fire. Emotions triggered by a story in and of itself are often intensified by the presence of likes, view counts, and user comments. The objectives below were created to help learners manage those emotions to move on to the crucial step of uncovering forensic clues to the information's credibility. This lesson will also help learners understand the difference between a primary and a secondary source in the digital age.

🐝 SEL Spotlight

One of the reasons traditional approaches to news literacy fail in their application outside of school is that our students haven't yet learned how to manage the emotional triggers embedded throughout their screen-filled lives. This case is unique in that it is designed to help learners recognize that even when the emotions triggered by information are positive (in this case, they make us feel superior to the people in the story who are calling 911 because they've run out of toilet paper), we should be wary of a response that causes us to let our credibility guard down. Additionally, this lesson offers Digital Detectives the opportunity to apply empathy toward the individuals who created and spread the false information. Even though the information was false, the intent of those spreading it was to change potentially harmful behavior. Make no mistake, this is not a justification for using online platforms to spread disinformation. However, thinking deeply about why someone might intentionally post content that is misleading or even downright false can help us better spot examples of this in the future. Through this lesson, we challenge learners to:

- Recognize when emotional triggers influence decisions made as Digital Detectives
- Examine how a shared trauma (like the COVID-19 pandemic) might influence both creators and consumers of information
- Consider their responsibility when sharing information that contains emotion-baiting content

Curricula Connections

Target Audience	6th–8th grade (As with all lessons in this book, this grade span is a suggestion only. With a few adaptations, this lesson could easily be applied to learners in other grades.)

Potential Content Area Connections/Collaborations

- Science: Pandemics, psychology, forensics
- ELA: Technical writing

ISTE Standards

Students

- Empowered Learner (1c): Students use technology to seek feedback that informs and improves their practice and to demonstrate their learning in a variety of ways.
- Knowledge Constructor (3b): Students evaluate the accuracy, perspective, credibility and relevance of information, media, data or other resources.
- Knowledge Constructor (3d): Students build knowledge by actively exploring real-world issues and problems, developing ideas and theories and pursuing answers and solutions.
- Computational Thinker (5c): Students break problems into component parts, extract key information, and develop descriptive models to understand complex systems or facilitate problem-solving.

Educators

- Citizen (3b): Educators establish a learning culture that promotes curiosity and critical examination of online resources and fosters digital literacy and media fluency.
- Designer (5b): Educators design authentic learning activities that align with content area standards and use digital tools and resources to maximize active, deep learning.
- Facilitator (6b): Educators manage the use of technology and student learning strategies in digital platforms, virtual environments, hands-on makerspaces or in the field.

Learning Objectives

By the end of this lesson:

- The learner will apply the Four Lenses to information as a step in determining credibility.
- The learner will apply the strategy of triangulation to determine information credibility.
- The learner will discover and explore a variety of motivations for creating false information.
- The learner will analyze the use of emotional triggers as a way to sensationalize and monetize information.
- The learner will develop and share a hypothesis related to information credibility.
- The learner will synthesize learning by creating an alternate outcome to the story shared in the case.

Resources Needed for This Lesson

Reminder: A variety of resources related to this chapter can be found in the Digital Detective's Evidence Locker. Use the QR code to the left, or visit evidencelocker.online. Then navigate to Chapter 9.

Time Needed for This Lesson: 2–4 hours

Case File

The following supplemental resources from the Digital Detective's Evidence Locker may be given to students to help them examine the case:

- [IMAGE] Hi-res version of the image shared in the student case file
- [ARTICLE] An Oregon Police Department Is Asking Residents to Stop Calling 911 Because They've Run Out of Toilet Paper
- [WEBSITE] Google Search for "Newport OR Police Department + Toilet Paper"
- [ARTICLE] Why Are People Hoarding Toilet Paper?

Process

1. Activating Prior Knowledge/Hook:

☑ Step/Tasks

a. Review the Four Lenses (see Chapters 1–4).
b. Review what students remember hearing about toilet paper shortages during the COVID-19 crisis.

◉ Suggested Resources

For this step, check in the Digital Detective's Evidence Locker for a link to:

- [VIDEO] Toilet Paper Shortages of the Early 2020s

2. Guided Practice Part 1: The Initial Hypothesis

☑ Step/Tasks

a. Working individually (or in pairs), have students review the one-sheet for The Case of . . . The 911 Toilet Paper Emergency!

b. As they review the case, students should record and classify clues related to the Four Lenses.
- ▶ Note: If you're using a traditional information literacy protocol (see Chapter 3) with students, now is the time to refer to it. However, remember that we recommend that these only be used as jumping-off points for learners: kindling to help spark their own investigations.

c. Product: By the end of this part of the lesson, student detective teams should generate an initial hypothesis or theory of the case.

d. Optional: Have students share their initial hypothesis with the group.

◉ Suggested Resources

For this step, check in the Digital Detective's Evidence Locker for:

- [TEMPLATE] Evidence Log (a tool that may support students as they detect and document clues from the case)
- [TEMPLATE] Case Synopsis (a tool that may support students as they present their final verdicts in the case)

3. Guided Practice Part 2: The Case File

☑ Step/Tasks

a. Give students access to selected items from the case file, noting that some of these items reveal the facts of the case.

b. Working in the same pairs and using the infographic Research Like a Fact Checker, have students work together to locate multiple sources that help to corroborate or contradict the story.
- ▶ Optional: The template Triangulation Talleys from the Digital Detective's Notebook may be used to record student findings.

🔘 Suggested Resources

For this step, check in the Digital Detective's Evidence Locker for:

- [INFOGRAPHIC] Research Like a Fact Checker
- [TEMPLATE] Triangulation Talley LOG

4. Assessment

☑ Step/Tasks

At this point, students should be ready to deliver a verdict on the case.

a. Individually, have students report their findings, including their final verdict regarding the story's credibility. Student responses can be recorded using the Case Synopsis template from the Digital Detective's Notebook or through a digital voting tool, such as Kahoot!, Poll Everywhere, or Socrative.

🔘 Suggested Resources

For this step, check in the Digital Detective's Evidence Locker for a link to:

- [TEMPLATE] Case Synopsis

5. Whole Group Debrief

☑ Step/Tasks

a. Together, as a whole group, have students debate the various theories of the case.
b. Together, classify clues students report into the Four Lenses.
   - ▶ Optional: This can be recorded using the Classified Evidence template from the Digital Detective's Notebook.
c. Have students identify which clues represented the "smoking gun" or pieces of evidence that ultimately convinced them the story was true or false.
d. Individually, or as a group, have students rate their own confidence in their verdict of the case.
   - ▶ Optional: We recommend using a Likert Scale for capturing this information. Digital tools such as Google Forms and Mentimeter are great options for creating this scale.

🔘 Suggested Resources

For this step, check in the Digital Detective's Evidence Locker for:

- [TEMPLATE] Classified Evidence
- [VIDEO] How to Use Likert Scales

6. Solution: Reveal the Facts of the Case! (See Below!)

☑ Step/Tasks

a. At this point, it's time to let students know where this story fell on the credibility spectrum. To do this, use the document The Facts of the Case (see the following section) to reveal the evidence associated with each lens that students should have uncovered.

b. We recommend that you also provide students with the opportunity to add evidence to the facts of the case. Students may have found other clues under each lens that can help their classmates think more deeply about credibility detection.

7. Synthesis

☑ Step/Tasks

To help students synthesize their learning, we want them to think more deeply about the motivations of those who created this false news story. Additionally, it is important for students to consider how the emotions associated with a global health crisis may have influenced both the creators of the story and those who believed it.

- Option 1: Have students create a press release written from the perspective of the Newport Police Department in which they address the evidence that was collected, who the suspect in the case was, and why they chose to create and share false information.
- Option 2: Have students create a video statement from the perspective of the Newport Police Department in which they address the evidence that was collected, who the suspect in the case was, and why they chose to create and share false information.
- Option 3: Have students create social media posts from concerned citizens, reacting to the news that the Newport Police Department planted this false story.

◉ Suggested Resources

For this step, check in the Digital Detective's Evidence Locker for links to:

- [DOCUMENT] Sample Press Release
- [VIDEO] How to Use Google Sheets to Generate Student Tweets

8. Reflection

☑ Step/Tasks

a. We recommend the 3-2-1 reflection protocol for this lesson:
   - ▶ Share the three most frustrating moments in the process of determining whether this story was true. Why were they frustrating?
   - ▶ Share two takeaways you'll remember from this lesson that can be used when you consume media in the future.
   - ▶ Assuming the Newport Police thought that, through the "blue lie" told on their Facebook page, they were serving their community by preventing potential strains on public resources, share one way that they might have accomplished this same goal without spreading false information. Bonus: How has the Newport Police Department's credibility been negatively affected, even though they were actually trying to do good?

9. Scaffolds

Chapters 1 and 3 offer mini-lessons that may be helpful as scaffolds for this unit.

- Finish This Comic! 1 (Chapter 1, Triggers)
- Emotional Trigger Bingo (Chapter 1, Triggers)
- From Emotion Triggers to Investigative Questions (Chapter 3, Forensics)

10. Potential Extensions

- Get into the mind of The Blue Liar! Have students consider:
  - ▶ What other big issues are people facing that a blue liar might want to change?
  - ▶ What kinds of false stories might a blue liar create in order to protect the public from this issue?
  - ▶ Have you ever been a blue liar? If so, what was the context and why did you feel justified in doing it? Looking back on it, would you do it again? Why or why not?
- Debate: Considering this story was fabricated, has the police department lost legitimacy with the community?
- Show clips from *The Office* (episode: "Product Recall"). Discuss connections to the 911 toilet paper story. What risks does The Blue Liar take when using the media to potentially change attitudes/outcomes?

Verdict **RED** | **FALSE** [Do Not Share]

Lens

LENS 1: TRIGGERS

Clues related to how elements of the story are designed to elicit, or trigger, an extreme emotional response.

Evidence

The Triggers Lens is critical to determining the facts of this case.

- Although we often think of an emotional trigger as inducing feelings of rage or fear, other emotions can also heavily influence our urge to believe or share information. This story relies on viewers feeling superior to the people calling 911.
- Additionally, because the story is linked to COVID-19, fear around the pandemic may also be triggered by the possibility that there may not be enough resources for everyone, and the police will be so busy dealing with nonsense that they won't be able to help people who are really in need.
- Viewers may have preexisting biases about the source(s) of the story.

Lens

LENS 2: ACCESS

Clues related to the device upon which the story is being viewed and how that access might change the way a Digital Detective locates evidence.

Evidence

- Access plays a role in our response to this story. Although we can see the source(s) of the story (CNN and Newport, OR, Police Dept.), social media as viewed on a mobile device does not immediately reveal authorship.
- The date published is not revealed through the Facebook app.
- Likes and other reactions from other viewers may influence our opinion of the story's credibility.

Lens

LENS 3: FORENSICS

Clues found in the details of the story, including (but not limited to) the URL, date published, authorship, and authority.

Evidence

- Triangulation is an important part of solving this case. Only by checking multiple sources might students discover that the Newport Police later clarified their statement, revealing that they had not received any 911 calls related to toilet paper shortages.
- Pointing students toward the article from *The Oregonian* will help them locate the clarification.

Lens

LENS 4: MOTIVES

Clues found in the motivations of potential suspects and how the story is created, shared, etc.

Evidence

- Though not a critical lens for this case, Motives provides an opportunity for interesting discussion.
- **Lineup:** If you choose to do a lineup activity for this lesson, we suggest the following suspects: The Jokester, The Mimicker, **The Blue Liar**, and The Conspiracy Theorist. Although The Blue Liar is, ultimately, the correct answer, students will be able to make a compelling case for The Jokester as well. The distinction will be that The Blue Liar's ultimate goal is to create social change.

CASE ONE-SHEET (MG) LESSON 9.2

The Case of . . . **Game! Set! Match! The Volleyball Playing Dog That Broke the Internet!**

The Scene

A video of a dog playing volleyball with her three human companions has taken the internet by storm!

In the footage, the talented canine can be seen perfectly striking the ball and helping her partner volley with players on the other side of the net.

Since first being shared, the video has been viewed over 100,000 times, receiving thousands of comments from both fans and skeptics alike. Some claim that the footage of the sporty pup brings new meaning to the phrase "man's best friend." Others point out that if the feel-good story looks "too good to be true," it probably is.

Possible Clues (Questions to Think About)

- **Triggers:** Is there anything about this story that makes us hope that it's true? Do those feelings influence our ability to determine what's real and what isn't?
- **Access:** Does the presence of comments and/or like and share counts affect your ability to determine fact from fiction?
- **Forensics:** How can we locate the original source of the information?
- **Motives:** If this story turns out to be false or misleading, what kind of person would create/spread it?

Is this story legit, or have people been served a foul?

💡 Big Ideas

This lesson focuses on the *Access* and *Triggers* Lenses. Details about the original source of the information are sparse, so learners will have to do some digging in order to find them. But will they want to? Even though (incredibly!) this story turns out to be true, there are numerous elements within the Community Reading Experience that may inspire doubt. In this case, the comments of other users, alongside an advertisement warning against manipulated videos may influence our work as Digital Detectives. The objectives below were designed to help learners think deeply about how the emotional triggers that often drive our decisions as information consumers are not limited to the information itself, and how the device through which we access information can play a role in exposing us to more of those triggers.

🦋 SEL Spotlight

Social media relies on the feeling of connection to thrive. Even though we might be alone in our rooms when we consume information in these spaces, we don't feel lonely, because we're sharing the experience with others online. This Community Reading Experience can allow us to learn about perspectives and opinions that differ from our own while also connecting us with potential experts or kindred spirits. On the other hand, the Community Reading Experience can also lead us to let our guard down as Digital Detectives when the consensus of the group seems united. If everyone who has viewed a story seems to believe (or disbelieve) it, that should give us pause, right? Well . . . maybe. In this lesson, the peripheral content surrounding the story itself all points to the story being false, even though it turns out to be true. By exploring this dichotomy, we hope to challenge learners to:

- Consider how emotional triggers can be embedded alongside information (and not just within it)
- Recognize when "group think" is influencing their work as Digital Detectives
- Develop strategies for going against the grain when the facts are on their side

Curricula Connections	
Target Audience	6th–8th grade (As with all lessons in this book, this grade span is a suggestion only. With a few adaptations, this lesson could easily be applied to other learners.)

Potential Content Area Connections/Collaborations

- Physical Education: Volleyball
- Math: Angles, scale factor
- ELA: Technical writing, creative writing, figurative language

ISTE Standards

Students

- Empowered Learner (1c): Students use technology to seek feedback that informs and improves their practice and to demonstrate their learning in a variety of ways.
- Digital Citizen (2a): Students cultivate and manage their digital identity and reputation and are aware of the permanence of their actions in the digital world.
- Knowledge Constructor (3b): Students evaluate the accuracy, perspective, credibility and relevance of information, media, data or other resources.
- Knowledge Constructor (3d): Students build knowledge by actively exploring real-world issues and problems, developing ideas and theories and pursuing answers and solutions.
- Computational Thinker (5c): Students break problems into component parts, extract key information, and develop descriptive models to understand complex systems or facilitate problem-solving.

Educators

- Citizen (3b): Educators establish a learning culture that promotes curiosity and critical examination of online resources and fosters digital literacy and media fluency.
- Designer (5b): Educators design authentic learning activities that align with content area standards and use digital tools and resources to maximize active, deep learning.
- Facilitator (6b): Educators manage technology and student learning strategies in digital platforms, virtual environments, hands-on makerspaces or in the field.

Learning Objectives

By the end of this lesson:

- The learner will apply the Four Lenses to information as a step in determining credibility.
- The learner will apply the strategy of triangulation to determine information credibility.
- The learner will discover and explore how the effect of the Community Reading Experience on social media affects our ability to determine credibility.
- The learner will identify the targeted advertisement in the information.
- The learner will develop and share a hypothesis related to information credibility.
- The learner will synthesize learning by creating an alternate outcome to the story shared in the case.

Resources Needed for This Lesson

Reminder: A variety of resources related to this chapter can be found in the Digital Detective's Evidence Locker. Use the QR code to the left, or visit evidencelocker.online. Then navigate to Chapter 9.

Time Needed for This Lesson: 2–4 hours

Case File

The following supplemental resources from Digital Detective's Evidence Locker may be given to students to examine the case:

- [IMAGE] Hi-res version of image shared in student case file
- [ARTICLE] This Insta-Popular Dog Playing Volleyball with Humans Is Breaking the Internet
- [ARTICLE] Beach Volleyball Player's Dog Becomes Social Media Sensation
- [WEBSITE] Kiara the dog's Instagram Profile
- [ARTICLE] Social Media Comments Can Impact Perceptions
- [VIDEO] Is the Internet Making Us Meaner?

Process

1. Activating Prior Knowledge/Hook:

☑ Step/Tasks

a. Review the Four Lenses (see Chapters 1–4).
b. Review what students know about video-based social media (such as Snapchat or TikTok). Have they ever seen an altered video on these sites?
   ▶ The infographic Seeing Is Believing. Or Is It? may be useful in completing this task.

🔘 Suggested Resources

For this step, check in the Digital Detective's Evidence Locker for a link to:

- [INFOGRAPHIC] Seeing Is Believing. Or Is It?

2. Guided Practice Part 1: The Initial Hypothesis

☑ Step/Tasks

a. Working individually (or in pairs), have students review the one-sheet for The Case of . . . Game! Set! Match! The Volleyball Playing Dog That Broke the Internet!

b. As they review the case, students should record and classify clues related to the Four Lenses.
  - ▶ Note: If you're using a traditional information literacy protocol (see Chapter 3) with students, now is the time to refer to it. However, remember that we recommend that these only be used as jumping-off points for learners: kindling to help spark their own investigations.

c. Product: By the end of this part of the lesson, student detective teams should generate an initial hypothesis or theory of the case.

d. Optional: Have students share their initial hypothesis with the group.

🔘 Suggested Resources

For this step, check in the Digital Detective's Evidence Locker for:

- [TEMPLATE] Evidence Log (a tool that may support students as they detect and document clues from the case)
- [TEMPLATE] Case Synopsis (a tool that may support students as they present their final verdicts in the case)

3. Guided Practice Part 2: The Case File

☑ Step/Tasks

a. Give students access to the rest of the case file. (Teachers should feel free to add other relevant items to the case file for students to review.)

b. Working in the same pairs, students should explore how the Community Reading Experience of accessing news on social media affects our reaction to news.
  - ▶ The Witness Statements template (from the Digital Detective's Notebook) may be helpful in completing this task.

🔘 Suggested Resources

For this step, check in the Digital Detective's Evidence Locker for:

- [TEMPLATE] Witness Statements
- [INFOGRAPHIC] What's Not to Like?

4. Assessment

☑ **Step/Tasks**

At this point, students should be ready to deliver a verdict on the case.

a. Individually, have students report their findings, including their final verdict regarding the story's credibility. Student responses can be recorded using the Case Synopsis template from the Digital Detective's Notebook or through a digital voting tool, such as Kahoot!, Poll Everywhere, or Socrative.

🔘 **Suggested Resources**

For this step, check in the Digital Detective's Evidence Locker for:

- [TEMPLATE] Case Synopsis

5. Whole Group Debrief

☑ **Step/Tasks**

a. Together, as a whole group, have students debate the various theories of the case.
b. Individually, or as a group, have students rate their own confidence in their verdict of the case.
   ▶ The Classified Evidence template from the Digital Detective's Notebook may be helpful in completing this task.

🔘 **Suggested Resources**

For this step, check in the Digital Detective's Evidence Locker for:

- [TEMPLATE] Classified Evidence

6. Solution: Reveal the Facts of the Case! (See Below!)

☑ **Step/Tasks**

a. At this point, it's time to let students know where this story fell on the credibility spectrum. To do this, use the document The Facts of the Case (see the following section) to reveal the evidence associated with each lens that students should have uncovered.
b. We recommend that you also provide students with the opportunity to add evidence to the facts of the case. Students may have found other clues under each lens that can help their classmates think more deeply about credibility detection.

7. Synthesis

☑ **Step/Tasks**

To help students synthesize their learning, we want them to think more deeply about how they contribute to the Community Reading Experience.

- Option 1: Using what they've learned from this lesson, have students craft a social media post supporting the credibility of this story—even though most other comments reveal that the rest of the community feels it is false.
- Option 2: Have students create their own targeted ad for this story that, based on what they know about the viewers/commentators, is guaranteed to get lots of clicks.

8. Reflection

☑ **Step/Tasks**

a. We recommend a variation on the "snowstorm" reflection activity for this.
   ► Students write down their biggest takeaway on a piece of scratch paper and wad it up. Given a signal, they "play volleyball" with a partner (using one of the responses at a time), by seeing if they can continue to volley the "ball" back and forth.
   ► When the ball hits the ground, the person to miss unravels and reads the response. Together they discuss the response until the teacher indicates that it's time for the next match or the end of the game.

9. Scaffolds

Chapters 1 and 2 offer mini-lessons that may be helpful as scaffolds for this unit.

- Fill in The Blanks—Community Reading Experience TAKE 1 (Chapter 2, Access)
- Finish This Comic! 2 (Chapter 2, Access)
- Emotional Trigger Bingo (Chapter 1, Triggers)

10. Potential Extensions

- Review the rules of volleyball. Have students rate Kiara's skills as specific moves.
- Have students consider other ways we use the word "peppering" and share how it can be used creatively to describe specific meanings.
- Rewrite this story from Kiara's perspective: How does she feel about her teammates? How does she feel about being a "social media sensation?" How do the comments in this story affect her?
- Use Dan Meyer's Three-Act Math strategy. Start the video when Kiara is hit by the volleyball, and ask them if it will make it over the net.

Verdict **GREEN** | **TRUE** [Share with Credit]

Lens

LENS 1: TRIGGERS

Clues related to how elements of the story are designed to elicit, or trigger, an extreme emotional response.

Evidence

- Although this story is true, readers may be influenced by negative comments in the feed. The number of comments speculating on the authenticity of the story, coupled with the advertising warning viewers about manipulated video, can serve as triggers that may influence student opinion of this story.
- Additionally, the "feel-good" nature of the story may influence how thoroughly students fact check.
- For this story, it's important for students to consider how this peripheral information might affect their perceptions.

Lens

LENS 2: ACCESS

Clues related to the device upon which the story is being viewed and how that access might change the way a Digital Detective locates evidence.

Evidence

- Although the handles of social media users who have shared this story are visible, the source or authorship of the article itself is not. It will be important for students to consider how to locate this information within the apps being used.
- Likes and other reactions from other viewers may influence student opinion of the story's credibility.
- Most importantly, however, the Community Reading Experience present in this story is an important aspect for readers to consider. While the information itself may lead learners to one conclusion, the peripheral comments and advertisements may cause them to think twice.

LENS 3: FORENSICS

Clues found in the details of the story, including (but not limited to) the URL, date published, authorship, and authority.

Evidence

- Triangulation is an important part of solving this case. Only by checking multiple sources might students discover the raw video footage.
- The case file for this story contains two different versions of the story. Students should consider the authority of each source and what makes one more credible than the other.

LENS 4: MOTIVES

Clues found in the motivations of potential suspects and how the story is created, shared, etc.

Evidence

- Although not a critical lens for this case, Motives provides an opportunity for interesting discussion.
- **Lineup:** If you choose to do a lineup activity for this lesson, we suggest the following suspects: The Mimicker, The Jokester, The Click Chaser, and The Influencer for Hire. Because this story is true, the correct answer will be **None of the Above**. However, students may make compelling arguments for any of these suspects.

The Case of . . . **The Superhuman Soldiers!**

The Scene

Have you seen this popular meme? With nearly 40,000 likes from this single Instagram post alone, it appears to be everywhere!

According to the meme, this photo was doctored and spread as propaganda to give the impression that Japanese soldiers were so strong they could lift a tank into the air. The meme also implies that the Japanese were able to accomplish this through some mysterious scientific discovery.

Although we know that no soldiers during World War II (from any country) were strong enough to lift a tank off the ground, what do you think? Did the Japanese really use this photo to fool Americans into thinking that they'd developed a superhuman army?

Possible Clues (Questions to Think About)

- **Triggers:** How does this information make you feel? Is there anything about how the information is presented that is designed to trigger an emotion?
- **Access:** Does the platform or app make it easier or more challenging to find additional information about the source?
- **Forensics:** How can you find out when/where this was originally published?
- **Motives:** If this story turns out to be false or misleading, what kind of person would create/spread it?

Do these soldiers really possess superhuman strength, or should this meme be tanked?

🔆 Big Ideas

This lesson focuses on the *Triggers* and *Access* Lenses. As a 2019 article from *The Washington Post* about memes being used as tools for recruiting young white males to white supremacy groups revealed (Gibson, 2019), these bite-sized bits of information are more than just funny images we text to our friends for a laugh. Indeed, as Stanford University historian and researcher Sam Wineburg demonstrated by tracing the journey of a racist meme on Twitter, the ubiquitous and non-threatening nature of memes makes them the perfect tool for spreading hate. His unpacking of how memes of this type play on our emotions, while also counting on readers who lack a basic understanding of history, was both fascinating and frightening (Wineburg, 2019). The objectives below were created to help learners look beyond the image and think about the design and wording choices of the creators of memes, while also considering how the ease of sharing contributes to the spread of disinformation in this form.

🔆 SEL Spotlight

Although the source of the original quote is a matter of speculation, we know for sure that the Motown classic "I Heard It Through the Grapevine" includes the lyrics "People say, 'believe half of what you see, son, and none of what you hear,'" a reference to the tried-and-true way that humans prioritize information. Even in the digital age, we tend to trust images over text alone. "Photographs furnish evidence," Susan Sontag wrote in *On Photography* (2011). "Something we hear about, but doubt, seems proven when we're shown a photograph of it." What we often fail to take into account, however, when making credibility decisions based on the "evidence" found in images, is what we bring to the table as humans whose experiences, memories, and biases affect how we view that image. Memes rely on evocative images, combined with sparse wording and specific design choices to trigger an emotion that makes us want to share. Sure, sometimes those emotions are rooted in humor and friendship. Other times, however, they are rooted in something darker and more dangerous. In this lesson, we challenge learners to:

- Recognize when design choices are made to trigger a specific emotion
- Identify ways to disrupt the community spread of disinformation

Curricula Connections

Target Audience	6th–8th grade (As with all lessons in this book, this grade span is a suggestion only. With a few adaptations, this lesson could easily be applied to other learners.)

Potential Content Area Connections/Collaborations

- Social Studies and Psychology: World War Two, propaganda
- Math: Coefficients, terms, variables, common measures of length and weight, force perspective

ISTE Standards

Students

- Empowered Learner (1c): Students use technology to seek feedback that informs and improves their practice and to demonstrate their learning in a variety of ways.
- Knowledge Constructor (3b): Students evaluate the accuracy, perspective, credibility and relevance of information, media, data or other resources.
- Knowledge Constructor (3d): Students build knowledge by actively exploring real-world issues and problems, developing ideas and theories and pursuing answers and solutions.
- Computational Thinker (5c): Students break problems into component parts, extract key information, and develop descriptive models to understand complex systems or facilitate problem-solving.

Educators

- Citizen (3b): Educators establish a learning culture that promotes curiosity and critical examination of online resources and fosters digital literacy and media fluency.
- Designer (5b): Educators design authentic learning activities that align with content area standards and use digital tools and resources to maximize active, deep learning.
- Facilitator (6b): Educators manage the use of technology and student learning strategies in digital platforms, virtual environments, hands-on makerspaces or in the field.

Learning Objectives

By the end of this lesson:

- The learner will apply the Four Lenses to information as a step in determining credibility.
- The learner will consider the relationship between historical context and propaganda in the modern world.
- The learner will explore how biases can be exploited to further an agenda.
- The learner will understand how memes can be used to spread misinformation.
- The learner will develop and share a hypothesis related to information credibility.
- The learner will synthesize learning by creating a meme exposing the historical context of the image used.

Resources Needed for This Lesson

Reminder: A variety of resources related to this chapter can be found in the Digital Detective's Evidence Locker. Use the QR code to the left, or visit evidencelocker.online. Then navigate to Chapter 9.

Time Needed for This Lesson: 2–4 hours

Case File

The following supplemental resources from Digital Detective's Evidence Locker may be given to students to help them examine the case. Be sure to note which resources for this story reveal the facts of the case.

- [IMAGE] Hi-res version of image shared in the case one-sheet
- [ARTICLE] Rumor Has It...And Rumor Has It Again!
- [VIDEO] Meme Warfare and Its Role in Propaganda
- [INFOGRAPHIC] It's Your Move! Knowing When Emotional Triggers Are Rigging the Game!

Process

1. Activating Prior Knowledge/Hook:

☑ Step/Tasks

a. Review the Four Lenses (see Chapters 1–4).
b. Review what students know about World War II. In particular, it will be important for students to understand which countries historians refer to as the Allied powers and which countries made up the Axis powers.
c. Review what students know about memes.

🔘 Suggested Resources

For this step, check in the Digital Detective's Evidence Locker for a link to:

- [WEBSITE] StoryCorps: Stories Featuring WWII Veterans

2. Guided Practice Part 1: The Initial Hypothesis

☑ Step/Tasks

a. Working individually (or in pairs), have students review the one-sheet for The Case of…The Superhuman Soldiers!
b. As they review the case, students should record and classify clues related to the Four Lenses.
  ▶ Note: If you're using a traditional information literacy protocol (see Chapter 3) with students, now is the time to refer to it. However, remember that we recommend that these only be used as jumping-off points for learners: kindling to help spark their own investigations.
c. Product: By the end of this part of the lesson, student detective teams should generate an initial hypothesis or theory of the case.
d. Optional: Have students share their initial hypothesis with the group.

🔘 Suggested Resources

For this step, check in the Digital Detective's Evidence Locker for:

- [TEMPLATE] Evidence Log (a tool that may support students as they detect and document clues from the case)
- [TEMPLATE] Case Synopsis (a tool that may support students as they present their final verdicts in the case)

3. Guided Practice Part 2: The Case File

☑ Step/Tasks

a. Give students access to selected items from the case file, noting that some of these items reveal the facts of the case.
b. Working in the same pairs, and using the Trigger Polygraph template, have students consider what strategies may have been used by the creator of the meme to trigger a strong emotional response in those viewing it.
  ▶ This may also be a good time to review how emotional triggers can affect our urge to trust/share information. Check the Evidence Locker for resources to support this work.

🌀 Suggested Resources

For this step, check in the Digital Detective's Evidence Locker for links to:

- [TEMPLATE] Trigger Polygraph
- [INFOGRAPHIC] It's Your Move! Knowing When Emotional Triggers Are Rigging the Game

4. Assessment

☑ Step/Tasks

At this point, students should be ready to deliver a verdict on the case.

a. Individually, have students report their findings, including their final verdict regarding the story's credibility.
   ▸ Student responses can be recorded using the Case Synopsis template from the Digital Detective's Notebook or through a digital voting tool, such as Kahoot!, Poll Everywhere, or Socrative.

🌀 Suggested Resources

For this step, check in the Digital Detective's Evidence Locker for:

- [TEMPLATE] Case Synopsis

5. Whole Group Debrief

☑ Step/Tasks

a. Together, as a whole group, have students debate the various theories of the case.
b. Together, classify clues students report into the Four Lenses.
   ▸ Optional: This can be recorded using the Classified Evidence template from the Digital Detective's Notebook.
c. Have students identify which clues represented the "smoking gun" or pieces of evidence that ultimately convinced them the story was true or false.
d. Individually, or as a group, have students rate their own confidence in their verdict of the case.
   ▸ We recommend using a Likert Scale for capturing this information. Digital tools such as Google Forms and Mentimeter are great options for creating this scale.

🌀 Suggested Resources

For this step, check in the Digital Detective's Evidence Locker for:

- [TEMPLATE] Classified Evidence

6. Solution: Reveal the Facts of the Case! (See Below!)

☑ **Step/Tasks**

a. At this point, it's time to let students know where this story fell on the credibility spectrum. To do this, use the document The Facts of the Case (see the following section) to reveal the evidence associated with each lens that students should have uncovered.

b. We recommend that you also provide students with the opportunity to add evidence to the facts of the case. Students may have found other clues under each lens that can help their classmates think more deeply about credibility detection.

7. Synthesis

☑ **Step/Tasks**

To help students synthesize their learning, we want them to think more deeply about how memes can be used to influence us as Digital Detectives.

- Option 1: Combat fire with fire! Have students create their own meme, utilizing some of the same tactics in the original, to reveal the truth!
- Option 2: Have students write a letter to themselves from the soldiers who were really responsible for creating the "ghost army." From the perspective of the soldiers, have students use the letter to describe how memes like this would make them feel about the ways their work is being used.

◉ Suggested Resources

For this step, check in the Digital Detective's Evidence Locker for links to:

- [INFOGRAPHIC] The Meme Made Me Do It
- [TEMPLATE] An Introduction to Letter Writing for Kids

8. Reflection

☑ **Step/Tasks**

a. Individually, have students consider how they've been triggered by information in the past.

b. Then, using the Finish This Comic! activity, have students illustrate how their own behavior will change in the future when they encounter information (including, but not limited to, memes) that has been designed to trigger them.

9. Scaffolds

Chapters 1 and 2 offer mini-lessons that may be helpful as scaffolds for this unit.

- Finish This Comic! 1 (Chapter 1, Triggers)
- Emotional Trigger Bingo (Chapter 1, Triggers)
- Finish This Comic! 2 (Chapter 2, Access)

10. Potential Extensions

- Have students create their own distorted images using forced perspective or simple photo editing software. Challenge students to create images that could fool someone into believing something that isn't true.

Verdict **RED** | **FALSE** [Do Not Share]

Lens

LENS 1: TRIGGERS

Clues related to how elements of the story are designed to elicit, or trigger, an extreme emotional response.

Evidence

- Although only implied, this meme is designed to make people suspicious of Asian Americans (specifically during the COVID-19 global health crisis).
- Language like *Japs* and *Asian enemies* and putting the word *science* in quotes are all designed to trigger an emotional response.
- These triggers might include existing feelings of prejudice or xenophobia, fear during a time of uncertainty, and/or distrust of science.

Lens

LENS 2: ACCESS

Clues related to the device upon which the story is being viewed and how that access might change the way a Digital Detective locates evidence.

Evidence

- This meme is being accessed through Instagram. This affects users' ability to easily view traditional clues such as:
  - ▶ Date of publication
  - ▶ Original source
- Students should think about how they would locate this information, along with other information about the source, were they really viewing it on a digital device.

Lens

LENS 3: FORENSICS

Clues found in the details of the story, including (but not limited to) the URL, date published, authorship, and authority.

Evidence

- The use of capital letters/bold font and multiple exclamation points at the end of sentences can be a clue that this was not created by a credible source.
- The date of publication can't be seen, and the listed location of the source also reflects a lack of authority.

Lens

LENS 4: MOTIVES

Clues found in the motivations of potential suspects and how the story is created, shared, etc.

Evidence

- This case offers a number of potential motives.
- **Lineup:** If you choose to do a lineup activity for this lesson, we suggest the following suspects: The Troll, The Outsider, The Wannabe, and **The Sentry**. While we created this lesson with The Sentry in mind, students will likely be able to create compelling arguments for all the suspects in the suggested lineup. Remember, there's no one right answer; rather, the goal is for Digital Detectives to recognize that the information shouldn't be shared or trusted.

The Case of . . . **The Reporter Who Risked Her Life for the News!**

The Scene

Reporters often put themselves in harm's way in order to keep the public informed, but this video takes that risk to an all-new level.

Filmed during a violent storm, the video depicts the reporter battling the wind and rain in order to show viewers how dangerous conditions really were. Then, just as the journalist is begging viewers to stay home and avoid all unnecessary travel, a rogue stop sign flies through the air, hitting the reporter in the head.

The video, which has millions of views on YouTube, was also shared millions more times on other social media platforms. But was it real?

Possible Clues (Questions to Think About)

- **Triggers:** Are there any potential triggers embedded in the headline? The chyron?
- **Access:** Does the format of the story affect its credibility or the ways we must detect clues?
- **Forensics:** How is "dusting for fingerprints" when the information is presented as a video different from when the information is presented in some other format?
- **Motives:** If this story turns out to be false or misleading, what kind of person would create/spread it?

Was this reporter seriously injured during a terrible storm, or is this post all wet?

💡 Big Ideas

This lesson focuses on the *Forensics* and *Motives* Lenses. There are a number of reasons that a person might create a video like the one in this case. While we ultimately identify this as a hoax, there's value in understanding how joke videos contain a financial incentive for its creator. The combination of sensational content coupled with a common, stressful experience (such as a major weather event) can prove extremely lucrative for content creators who monetize their YouTube channels (or other platforms). While the goal of this video might appear to be humorous, it's noteworthy that, despite the fact that it is false, it actually raised the social capital of the reporter: She became the subject of numerous memes, as well as news stories about how her report on this storm went viral in an unexpected way. As people from around the world clicked to learn more, they invariably also added to the view counts of the individuals who created the hoax content to begin with. The objectives below were created to help learners not only sharpen their skills at detecting altered video content but also serve as a reminder of how viral videos incentivize the creation of false content.

🦋 SEL Spotlight

Extreme weather events (such as this mega storm) are often used as fodder for those wishing to spread false information, especially in the form of video. Videos featuring sharks invading city streets or millions of crabs crossing the road are a familiar marker of hurricane season. Why is this? Sometimes these videos are obviously just harmless hoaxes, turning a frightening and dangerous event into something we can all laugh about. Other times, the videos are more convincing and add to our collective anxiety around the event. Occasionally, these altered weather reports are used to spread an agenda related to climate change or government policy around natural resources. Knowing how to spot when a video may be altered is an important skill for today's digital learners to master. However, as the tools used to create suspect content become more advanced, digital tells will become even harder to spot. On the other hand, recognizing when a video (or any information) has triggered a strong emotional response is a skill that will serve learners well, regardless of how skilled video editors become at creating content that is designed to fool us. In this lesson, we challenge learners to:

- Recognize when emotional triggers influence decisions made as Digital Detectives
- Understand how video, audio, and text can work together to form a "mega storm" of emotional triggers that we all should be wary of

Curricula Connections	
Target Audience	6th–8th grade (As with all lessons in this book, this grade span is a suggestion only. With a few adaptations, this lesson could easily be applied to other learners.)

Potential Content Area Connections/Collaborations

- Science: Weather and climate

ISTE Standards

Students

- Digital Citizen (2b): Students engage in positive, safe, legal and ethical behavior when using technology, including social interactions online or when using networked devices.
- Knowledge Constructor (3b): Students evaluate the accuracy, perspective, credibility and relevance of information, media, data or other resources.
- Knowledge Constructor (3d): Students build knowledge by actively exploring real-world issues and problems, developing ideas and theories and pursuing answers and solutions.
- Creative Communicator (6c): Students communicate complex ideas clearly and effectively by creating or using various digital objects such as visualizations, models or simulations.

Educators

- Citizen (3b): Educators establish a learning culture that promotes curiosity and critical examination of online resources and fosters digital literacy and media fluency.
- Citizen (3c): Educators mentor students in safe, legal and ethical practices with digital tools and the protection of intellectual rights and property.
- Designer (5b): Educators design authentic learning activities that align with content area standards and use digital tools and resources to maximize active, deep learning.

Learning Objectives

By the end of this lesson:

- The learner will apply the Four Lenses to information as a step in determining credibility.
- The learner will explore ways in which videos can be altered to fool viewers.
- The learner will understand the concept of hoax news.
- The learner will consider the motivations of individuals who create hoax information.
- The learner will develop and share a hypothesis related to information credibility.
- The learner will synthesize learning by creating altered images/videos.

Resources Needed for This Lesson

Reminder: A variety of resources related to this chapter can be found in the Digital Detective's Evidence Locker. Use the QR code to the left, or visit evidencelocker.online. Then navigate to Chapter 9.

Time Needed for This Lesson: 2–4 hours

Case File

The following supplemental resources from Digital Detective's Evidence Locker may be given to students to help them examine the case. Be sure to note which resources for this story reveal the facts of the case.

- [IMAGE] Hi-res version of image shared in the case one-sheet
- [ARTICLE] How to Change the Impression of Space and Depth Within a Scene
- [INFOGRAPHIC] Tips for Spotting Fake Videos Online
- [ARTICLE] 10 Tips for Verifying Viral Social Media Videos
- [ARTICLE] Breaking News Reports Can Be Hit-or-Miss, Because Accuracy Takes Time

Process

1. Activating Prior Knowledge/Hook:

☑ Step/Tasks

a. Review the Four Lenses (see Chapters 1–4).
b. Review what students know about major weather events. Ask them to identify the names of storms that they remember.
   ▶ We recommend the digital tool Mentimeter as a possible option for completing this task.
c. Alternately, show a brief clip from the film *The Day After Tomorrow* and have students consider why, even though they know this is imagined, scenarios like those depicted in the film are so frightening.

◉ Suggested Resources

For this step, check in the Digital Detective's Evidence Locker for links to:

- [VIDEO] Tutorial for Mentimeter
- [VIDEO] Clip from *The Day After Tomorrow*

2. Guided Practice Part 1: The Initial Hypothesis

☑ Step/Tasks

a. Working individually (or in pairs), have students review the one-sheet for The Case of . . . The Reporter Who Risked Her Life for the News!
b. As they review the case, students should record and classify clues related to the Four Lenses.
   ▶ Note: If you're using a traditional information literacy protocol (see Chapter 3) with students, now is the time to refer to it. However, remember that we recommend that these only be used as jumping-off points for learners: kindling to help spark their own investigations.
c. Product: By the end of this part of the lesson, student detective teams should generate an initial hypothesis or theory of the case.
d. Optional: Have students share their initial hypothesis with the group.

◉ Suggested Resources

For this step, check in the Digital Detective's Evidence Locker for:

- [TEMPLATE] Evidence Log (a tool that may support students as they detect and document clues from the case)
- [TEMPLATE] Case Synopsis (a tool that may support students as they present their final verdicts in the case)

3. Guided Practice Part 2: The Case File

✅ Step/Tasks

a. Give students access to selected items from the case file, noting that some of these items reveal the facts of the case.
b. Working in the same pairs, and using the infographic Tips for Spotting Fake Videos Online (from the case file), students should consider what, if any, aspects of the video are potential credibility red flags.

🔎 Suggested Resources

For this step, check in the Digital Detective's Evidence Locker for a link to:

- [INFOGRAPHIC] Tips for Spotting Fake Videos Online

4. Assessment

✅ Step/Tasks

At this point, students should be ready to deliver a verdict on the case.

a. Individually, have students report their findings, including their final verdict regarding the story's credibility.
  ▶ Student responses can be recorded using the Case Synopsis template from the Digital Detective's Notebook or through a digital voting tool, such as Kahoot!, Poll Everywhere, or Socrative.

🔎 Suggested Resources

For this step, check in the Digital Detective's Evidence Locker for:

- [TEMPLATE] Case Synopsis

5. Whole Group Debrief

✅ Step/Tasks

a. Together, as a whole group, have students debate the various theories of the case.
b. Together, classify clues students report into the Four Lenses.
  ▶ Optional: This can be recorded using the Classified Evidence template from the Digital Detective's Notebook.
c. Have students identify which clues represented the "smoking gun" or pieces of evidence that ultimately convinced them the story was true or false.
d. Individually, or as a group, have students rate their own confidence in their verdict of the case.
  ▶ We recommend using a Likert Scale for capturing this information. Digital tools such as Google Forms and Mentimeter are great options for creating this scale.

🌀 Suggested Resources

For this step, check in the Digital Detective's Evidence Locker for:

- [TEMPLATE] Classified Evidence

6. Solution: Reveal the Facts of the Case! (See Below!)

☑ Step/Tasks

a. At this point, it's time to let students know where this story fell on the credibility spectrum. To do this, use the document The Facts of the Case (see the following section) to reveal the evidence associated with each lens that students should have uncovered.
b. We recommend that you also provide students with the opportunity to add evidence to the facts of the case. Students may have found other clues under each lens that can help their classmates think more deeply about credibility detection.

7. Synthesis

☑ Step/Tasks

To help students synthesize their learning, we want them to think more deeply about how easy it is to alter videos.

- Option 1:
  - ▶ Working in teams, and using the tool of their choice, have students create their own altered photos or videos along with a misleading headline.
  - ▶ Using a digital tool like Padlet, have students share their creations.
  - ▶ Finally, have students leave feedback for their classmates noting that while feedback should be both responsible and constructive, it should also address one "glow" and one "grow." A glow refers to one exceptional part of students' final products, whereas a grow refers to one part of the final product that could be improved.
- Option 2 (can be completed separately, or as part of Option 1):
  - ▶ Using the infographic Follow the Money, have students identify all four players (who in this case is the creator? The host?) in the relationship between clicks and money. Then have them identify who, on that list, has the most incentive to share false information and who, by contrast, has the most power to stop its spread.
    - Note: Chapter 8's The Case of . . . The 450lb Dog! Resources may be helpful as either a complement or a review for this lesson.

🌀 Suggested Resources

For this step, check in the Digital Detective's Evidence Locker for links to:

- Potential tools for creating altered photos/videos
- [VIDEO] Tutorial for Padlet
- [INFOGRAPHIC] Follow the Money!

8. Reflection

☑ Step/Tasks

a. We recommend the "triangle, square, circle" reflection protocol for this activity. In this protocol the teacher draws a triangle, a square, and a circle on the board. Each contains a different question:
   - ► Triangle: What did I learn from this activity?
   - ► Square: Why does this learning matter?
   - ► Circle: If I decide to share a hoax video in the future, how should I craft my posts so that others also know that it is a hoax?

b. The teacher can then assign specific shapes/questions to individual learners, randomly select a shape using a digital randomizer, or have students select which question they want to respond to.

c. If available, sticky notes in the three shapes can be used to collect student responses.

d. Alternately, if available, students can share their responses on large poster paper containing the three shapes. This both encourages movement and gives students the opportunity to view other perspectives.

9. Scaffolds

Chapters 3 and 4 offer mini-lessons that may be helpful as scaffolds for this unit.

- Asking the Right Questions Jamboard (Chapter 3, Forensics)
- From Emotional Triggers to Investigative Questions (Chapter 3, Forensics)
- Mis Dis or Mal Information—Matching Game (Chapter 4, Motives)

10. Potential Extensions

- Using a list of recently named mega storms from around the world, have students locate hoax videos that go along with each storm. Students can then reflect on why natural disasters inspire this type of false information online.
  - ► Take this one step further and have students map the storms and associated videos using Google Earth, creating a tour of extreme weather phenomenon and the hoax videos they inspire from around the world.
  - ► Once complete, students could then review all the content to create a list of characteristics all or a majority of the hoax videos have in common.

THE FACTS OF THE CASE

Verdict **YELLOW: FALSE** (but Not Harmful) [Share Only with Explanation]

Lens

LENS 1: TRIGGERS

Clues related to how elements of the story are designed to elicit, or trigger, an extreme emotional response.

Evidence

- While, ultimately, this story is a hoax and meant to be humorous, some viewers might be triggered by the presence of potential danger, both for the reporter and for people who may be affected by the "mega storm."
- Language like *breaking news* can also elicit an emotional response because it implies that the situation requires urgent attention or something to be fearful of.

Lens

LENS 2: ACCESS

Clues related to the device upon which the story is being viewed and how that access might change the way a Digital Detective locates evidence.

Evidence

- When viewed on a mobile device, the YouTube app adds layers to the process of determining credibility.
  - ▶ Viewers must click an unmarked arrow next to the title of the video in order to view information such as the date of publication or the category in which the video is featured.
  - ▶ Similarly, the YouTube app defaults to displaying "top comments" first, which can affect whether potentially helpful information shared by viewers is seen at all.
  - ▶ Although created for TV, this story ultimately went viral on social media. Seeing the clicks as a video is seen and shared can influence how we view credibility. Additionally, viral stories are repeated in our feeds, which can influence our view of the information.

Lens

LENS 3: FORENSICS

Clues found in the details of the story, including (but not limited to) the URL, date published, authorship, and authority.

Evidence

- It's often tempting to accept video as irrefutable evidence, but seeing isn't always believing. In this story, there are several digital fingerprints that can help students determine credibility:
  - ▶ Audio of the crash sound, while jarring, does not match the remaining audio's volume.
  - ▶ The scale of the stop sign is incorrect. An actual stop sign would be much larger than the reporter's face.
  - ▶ "Smoking stop sign" does not represent what would really happen.
  - ▶ We don't see the reporter fall; she simply disappears.
  - ▶ The source posting the video is not a journalistic outlet.
  - ▶ Video is posted in the "comedy" category.

Lens

LENS 4: MOTIVES

Clues found in the motivations of potential suspects and how the story is created, shared, etc.

Evidence

- This video is a hoax and is intended to be humorous.
- **Lineup:** If you choose to do a lineup activity for this lesson, we suggest the following suspects: The Wannabe, **The Jokester,** The Click Chaser, and The Doppelgänger. While The Jokester is, ultimately, the correct answer, students will be able to make a compelling case for The Click Chaser as well. Remember, there's no one right answer; rather, the goal is for Digital Detectives to recognize that the information shouldn't be shared or trusted.

Digital Detective's Lessons for High School Learners

This chapter consists of four lessons designed to help high school learners assume the role of Digital Detective by applying the Four Lenses to a broad array of news stories from various information sources.

These lessons are supported by tools and resources to help you implement them as soon as you feel your Digital Detectives are ready to start cracking cases. As noted earlier, we encourage you to think outside the grade spans we've identified. For example, if you teach high school learners, we hope you'll explore the cases designed for both elementary and middle grade learners, too. With your experience brought to bear, we're betting some of those lessons could be reworked for your Digital Detectives as well.

Contents

The Case of . . . **The Girl on Fire!**

The Scene

Love it or hate it, twerking is a fad that seems to be here to stay. Those who dislike the provocative dance move, however, have found an example of why twerking should be banned in this video.

Although initially intended to impress the subject's boyfriend, it appears to depict a chaotic scene in which romance quickly turns to terror as her hopes, and pants, go up in flames!

With well over 2 million views on social media, this video has also been picked up by news outlets ranging from Fox News to MSNBC to The View, with several commentators warning parents to talk to their kids about the dangers of twerking.

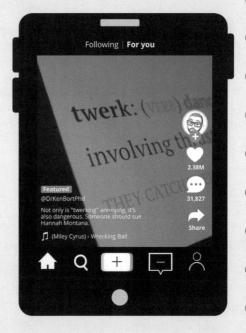

Possible Clues (Questions to Think About)

- **Triggers:** How does this information make you feel about the people involved? Does that play a role in making you want to like/share it?
- **Access:** Does the app being used make it easier or more difficult to locate the primary versus the secondary source?

- **Forensics:** How can we locate the original source of the information?
- **Motives:** If this story turns out to be false or misleading, what kind of person would create/spread it?

Is seeing believing, or are this liar's pants really on fire?

Big Ideas

This lesson focuses on the *Motives* and *Triggers* Lenses. While we often encourage learners to be wary of information that triggers a negative response (such as fear or anger), it's also vital for them to recognize how any extreme emotional response should be viewed as a credibility red flag. "How does this information make me feel?" and "Do these feelings affect my urge to share this information without checking it out further?" should be the first questions we ask ourselves when considering whether something is real. Emotion as the driver of action is an outcome false information–creators count on. Embedding emotionally triggering information is an effective way to create viral content. The objectives below were designed to help learners interrogate the idea that while there are many different motives for creating false information, carefully crafted emotional triggers are a common tactic used to achieve them.

SEL Spotlight

Perhaps more than in any other time in human history, the information we consume and share has become a part of our identity. The filter bubbles we surround ourselves with confirm the messages we internalize, which then help shape who we believe we are and who we hope to become. Today's learners are no different, crafting detailed biographies for social media profiles featuring Facetuned headshots and idealized avatars. We spend a lot of time helping kids understand their digital footprints, not only as consumers of but also as creators and conduits of information. As teens develop a height-ened sense of identity, which includes increased attention paid to how others perceive them and how they perceive themselves, understanding the connec-tion between their digital lives and their own identity can be powerful. While there's an urge to think of the time we spend online versus that spent "IRL" (in real life) as separate and disparate, the truth is that these worlds are overlap-ping and reciprocal. Older learners are not only capable of understanding this relationship, but can also be motivated by that knowledge as we help them develop habits and strategies for navigating in healthy and productive ways. Through these activities, we encourage learners to:

- Recognize emotional triggers as a red flag
- Understand how sharing false information affects their credibility
- Consider their role as an information creator and conduit

Curricula Connections

Target Audience	9th–12th (As with all lessons in this book, this grade span is a suggestion only. With a few adaptations, this lesson could easily be applied to other learners.)

Potential Content Area Connections/Collaborations

- Health/Psychology: Emotions, emotional intelligence, executive functioning
- Sociology: How groups of people are influenced
- History: History of dance
- Economics: Consumers
- ELA: Elements of story, storyboarding
- CTE: Business, marketing

ISTE Standards

Students

- Empowered Learner (1c): Students use technology to seek feedback that informs and improves their practice and to demonstrate their learning in a variety of ways.
- Knowledge Constructor (3b): Students evaluate the accuracy, perspective, credibility and relevance of information, media, data or other resources.
- Knowledge Constructor (3d): Students build knowledge by actively exploring real-world issues and problems, developing ideas and theories and pursuing answers and solutions.
- Computational Thinker (5c): Students break problems into component parts, extract key information, and develop descriptive models to understand complex systems or facilitate problem-solving.

Educators

- Citizen (3b): Educators establish a learning culture that promotes curiosity and critical examination of online resources and fosters digital literacy and media fluency.
- Designer (5b): Educators design authentic learning activities that align with content area standards and use digital tools and resources to maximize active, deep learning.
- Facilitator (6b): Educators manage the use of technology and student learning strategies in digital platforms, virtual environments, hands-on makerspaces or in the field.
- Analyst (7a): Educators provide alternative ways for students to demonstrate competency and reflect on their learning using technology.

Learning Objectives

By the end of this lesson:

- The learner will apply the Four Lenses to information as a step in determining credibility.
- The learner will analyze the motivations of people who post false content online.
- The learner will explore the ways that emotional triggers in information can affect the urge to share.
- The learner will identify the emotional triggers that they are most vulnerable to as information consumers.
- The learner will evaluate strategies for leveraging emotional triggers to create viral content.
- The learner will synthesize learning by creating an advertising plan that leverages triggers to drive click-based revenue.

Resources Needed for This Lesson

Reminder: A variety of resources related to this chapter can be found in the Digital Detective's Evidence Locker. Use the QR code to the left, or visit evidencelocker.online. Then navigate to Chapter 10.

Time Needed for This Lesson: 2–4 hours

Case File

The following supplemental resources from the Digital Detective's Evidence Locker may be given to students to examine the case. Be sure to note which resources for this story reveal the facts of the case.

- [IMAGE] Hi-res version of the image shared in the student one-sheet
- [ARTICLE w/ VIDEO] Viral Video: When Twerking Gets Dangerous
- [ARTICLE w/ VIDEO] Girl Sets Herself on Fire While Twerking
- [INFOGRAPHIC] It's Your Move: When Emotional Triggers Rig the Game
- [ARTICLE] What Do Twerking and the Charleston Have in Common?

Process

1. Activating Prior Knowledge/Hook:

☑ Step/Tasks

a. Review the Four Lenses (see Chapters 1–4).
b. Have students share what they know about emotional triggers.
c. Using a digital voting tool (like Dotstorming), have students share and then "vote up" the emotions (anger, fear, outrage, etc.) they feel are most often triggered by information.

⊚ Suggested Resources

For this step, check in the Digital Detective's Evidence Locker for links to:

- [VIDEO] Tutorial for Using Dotstorming
- [VIDEO] How Emotions Affect Our Brain

2. Guided Practice Part 1: The Initial Hypothesis

☑ Step/Tasks

a. Working individually (or in pairs), have students review the one-sheet for The Case of . . . The Girl on Fire!
b. As they review the case, students should record and classify clues related to the Four Lenses.
   ▶ Note: If you're using a traditional information literacy protocol (see Chapter 3) with students, now is the time to refer to it. However, remember that we recommend that these only be used as jumping-off points for learners: kindling to help spark their own investigations.
c. Product: By the end of this part of the lesson, student detective teams should generate an initial hypothesis or theory of the case.
d. Optional: Have students share their initial hypothesis with the group.

⊚ Suggested Resources

For this step, check in the Digital Detective's Evidence Locker for:

- [TEMPLATE] Evidence Log (a tool that may support students as they detect and document clues from the case)
- [TEMPLATE] Case Synopsis (a tool that may support students as they present their final verdicts in the case)

3. Guided Practice Part 2: The Case File

☑ Step/Tasks

a. Give students access to selected items from the case file, noting that some of these items reveal the facts of the case.
b. Working in the same pairs and using the infographic It's Your Move, have students:
   ▶ First, create a list of synonyms for the Big Seven emotions.
   ▶ Next, have students consider which of those emotions might be triggered by the video.
   ▶ Finally, discuss the following questions: Were you to share this video, which of the Big Seven do you think would be triggered in your friends, family, and/or community? Do you think members of your network would share the video themselves? Why or why not?

⊚ Suggested Resources

For this step, check in the Digital Detective's Evidence Locker for a link to:

- [INFOGRAPHIC] Tips for Spotting Fake Videos Online

4. Assessment

☑ Step/Tasks

At this point, students should be ready to deliver a verdict on the case.

a. Individually, have students report their findings, including their final verdict regarding the story's credibility. Student responses can be recorded using the Case Synopsis template from the Digital Detective's Notebook or through a digital voting tool, such as Kahoot!, Poll Everywhere, or Socrative.

⊚ Suggested Resources

For this step, check in the Digital Detective's Evidence Locker for:

- [TEMPLATE] Case Synopsis

5. Whole Group Debrief

☑ Step/Tasks

a. Together, as a whole group, have students debate the various theories of the case.
b. Individually or as a group, have students rate their own confidence in their verdict of the case.
   ▶ We recommend using a Likert Scale for capturing this information. Digital tools such as Google Forms and Mentimeter are great options for creating this scale.

◉ Suggested Resources

For this step, check in the Digital Detective's Evidence Locker for:

- [VIDEO] How to Use Likert Scales

6. Solution: Reveal the Facts of the Case! (See Below!)

☑ Step/Tasks

a. At this point, it's time to let students know where this story fell on the credibility spectrum. To do this, use the document The Facts of the Case (see the following section) to reveal the evidence associated with each lens that students should have uncovered.
b. We recommend that you also provide students the opportunity to add evidence to the facts of the case. Students may have found other clues under each lens that can help their classmates think more deeply about credibility detection.

7. Synthesis

☑ Step/Tasks

To help students synthesize their learning, we want them to think more deeply about how emotional triggers can lead to financial reward for content creators.

a. Working in small groups, have students use what they know about emotional triggers and the infographic Native Advertising to develop a marketing plan that capitalizes on the emotions triggered by the video.
b. Prior to getting started, have students consider the motivations of the person crafting this plan. Assign each group a suspect from Chapter 2. Possible examples include: The Sock Puppet, The Click Chaser, The Operative, The Influencer for Hire, and The Activist. Remind them that their ad campaign should be designed to achieve the goal of the suspect they've been assigned, whose motivations should inform all of their decisions.

▶ Note: In addition to understanding the different types of native advertising, this is an opportunity for learners to consider *when* in the video the ad should appear. We recommend using a storyboarding tool (like Storyboard That) to help students illustrate specific moments in the video that lend themselves to different native advertising strategies.

▶ For an added challenge, ask students to include attempts at triggering as many of the Big Seven emotions as possible in their ad plan.

c. Using a collaborative brainstorming tool, such as Padlet, have students share their final plans, along with a short narrative explaining what elements they most want their classmates to take note of.

▶ You may choose to have students reveal which suspect created this advertising plan, or you may choose to have the class guess.

d. Using the commenting features in Padlet, have students comment on one another's work. We recommend a modified version of the "tuning" feedback protocol, in which students share their work with their peers, take questions, and receive feedback and suggestions for further fine-tuning.

🔘 Suggested Resources

For this step, check in the Digital Detective's Evidence Locker for links to:

- [INFOGRAPHIC] Native Advertising
- [WEBSITE] Tutorial for Storyboard That
- [VIDEO] Tutorial for Padlet
- Information about the "tuning" feedback protocol

8. Reflection

a. We recommend the Hear, Think, and Do reflection as an extension of the tuning protocol. For this activity, have students add to their advertising plan with a final frame or slide in which they depict themselves:

▶ *Hearing* specific feedback from their peers

▶ *Thinking* about or processing that feedback

▶ *Doing* or taking next steps to make their project better based on what they heard from their classmates

9. Scaffolds

Chapters 1 and 4 offer mini-lessons that may be helpful as scaffolds for this unit.

- Heads Up Game—Version 2 (Chapter 4, Motives)
- Mis Dis or Mal Information—Matching Game (Chapter 4, Motives)
- Information Literacy Identity Webs (Chapter 1, Triggers)

10. Potential Extensions

- At the beginning of this lesson, ask students to consider what might happen if they shared this video in their networks without context and to predict what emotions might be experienced by their friends, families, and communities as a result. As an extension, students could create a survey to go along with this video that asks participants to identify emotions triggered by the video and/or information in general. After developing and distributing the survey, have students compare the results against their initial predictions. Finally, have students use that data to inform potential changes to the advertising plan they crafted with their classmates.

Verdict **YELLOW | FALSE** (but Not Harmful) [Share Only with Explanation]

Lens

LENS 1: TRIGGERS

Clues related to how elements of the story are designed to elicit, or trigger, an extreme emotional response.

Evidence

- Triggers is the most significant lens when considering the credibility of this story. As the reveal video explains, TV personality Jimmy Kimmel posted the twerking video on YouTube but did nothing else except wait for "the internet to work its magic." Without any promotion, the video received several million hits and triggered an avalanche of spinoff stories from all sorts of media, many of which warned of the dangers of twerking.
- For this lesson, it is vital for learners to think about what emotions drive that response to the video. Potential conversations may be had around the following emotions:
  - ▶ Fear/worry: Parents or other adults may feel fear related to the welfare of their teenage children.
  - ▶ Flattery: Some people viewing the video may feel superior to the people in it; this is a form of flattery. When information makes you feel smarter or better than the people involved, it may be pandering to your ego.
  - ▶ Envy: Some viewers might be envious of the fame experienced by those in it.

Lens

LENS 2: ACCESS

Clues related to the device upon which the story is being viewed and how that access might change the way a Digital Detective locates evidence.

Evidence

- Although not the primary lens through which this story is viewed, Access does play a role in how we determine credibility. Apps like TikTok strengthen our emotional response to information through the Community Reading Experience. Like and share counts, along with our proximity to the person sharing information, can all affect our urge to like or share it without thorough investigation.

Lens

LENS 3: FORENSICS

Clues found in the details of the story, including (but not limited to) the URL, date published, authorship, and authority.

Evidence

- Although not the primary lens through which this story is viewed, there are a couple of forensic clues that students may pick up when analyzing this case.
  - ▶ The fact that the camera remains steady throughout the fall may be a clue indicating a professional setup.
  - ▶ The fact that the profile of the person sharing the video (on YouTube) contains no biographical information and this video is their only post may also be a credibility red flag.

Lens

LENS 4: MOTIVES

Clues found in the motivations of potential suspects and how the story is created, shared, etc.

Evidence

- The Motives Lens is another important one through which students should view this post. Although we know that the video was a hoax, and contained no native advertising, this provides learners with the opportunity to consider how that advertising might be crafted depending on the motives of the individual sharing.
- **Lineup:** If you choose to do a lineup activity for this lesson, we suggest the following suspects: The Influencer for Hire, The Stan, The Lemming, and **The Jokester.** While we created this lesson with The Jokester in mind, students will likely be able to create compelling arguments for all the suspects in the suggested lineup. Remember, there's no one right answer; rather, the goal is for Digital Detectives to recognize that the information shouldn't be shared or trusted.

The case of . . . **The Pillow Fight Pact!**

The Scene

Troubled by data suggesting that enrollment at the U.S. Military Academy at West Point is in decline, first-year cadets took matters into their own hands.

As many as 60 first-year cadets (roughly 25% of the class), known as plebes, allegedly took part in a "pregnancy pact," vowing to get their girlfriends pregnant before the end of the year so that their future children could attend West Point and boost enrollment. In a bizarre twist, the plebes decided to use the annual first-year cadet pillow fight as the arena for publicly declaring their intent.

Annual West Point Pillow Fight Banned After Cadets Use Long-Time Tradition As Front For Pregnancy Pledge.

2.2M views · 1 year ago

67K   837   Share   Download   Save

MILITARY NEWS   SUBSCRIBE
6.84M subscribers

Comments 3.6K

Someone needs to loose their job over this. I hope these cadets loose their commissions after this...

Speaking on condition of anonymity, one cadet said, "The deal was that you had to draw blood at the pillow fight to show you were all in on the pact. If you didn't give someone a bloody nose or a concussion, you didn't try hard enough for your school." Another revealed, "We were breaking the code of conduct, but we were following a higher one."

Possible Clues (Questions to Think About)

- **Triggers:** How does this information make you feel about the people involved?
- **Access:** Does the app being used make it easier or more difficult to determine credibility?
- **Forensics:** Are there clues in the information itself that can help us determine credibility?
- **Motives:** If this story turns out to be false or misleading, what kind of person would create/spread it?

Is this story about giving West Point a baby boost true, or is this pillow full of feathers?

💡 Big Ideas

This lesson focuses on the *Forensics* and *Triggers* Lenses. We tend to think about the news as being entirely right or entirely false. However, false information creators know that the perfect recipe for fooling information consumers typically contains a dash of fact. Data and/or context manipulation are frequently and effectively used strategies for spreading false information rooted, at least in part, in truth. Take, for example, all those videos that pop up whenever there's a natural disaster, featuring sharks swimming down a city street or tens of thousands of crabs descending on a suburban town. One of the reasons those hoaxes tend to fool people is that at least some of the story's details are true. The video of all those crabs, for example, is likely real footage that was taken of a natural, migratory event, rather than during a natural disaster. By mislabeling it or changing the context, unscrupulous content creators can stoke panic, heighten emotion, and ultimately, make more money by getting us to click. Data can be similarly manipulated to convey partial truths or incomplete pictures. Emphasizing some data points rather than others, or linking factual data to unrelated events, are common tactics for those who wish to use numbers to influence or manipulate. In this lesson, we want to help students think deeply about context and data. The objectives below were created to help learners understand the different ways small pieces of information can be manipulated to make us believe much bigger falsehoods.

🐝 SEL Spotlight

As we mentioned in Chapter 3, the average person spends only about eight seconds evaluating a piece of information before deciding to trust or share it. The human brain can process only so much information in that small amount of time. Even if we click past the headline to dig a little deeper, our minds scan for information we can trust and then looks to affirm our beliefs or information that raises a credibility red flag. Data often represents the former. Phrases like "trust the numbers" or "numbers don't lie" have added to the belief that data is neutral; if there's data to support a claim, that claim must be valid, and by extension, information that contains supporting data must be trustworthy. Right? Well . . . not exactly. In this lesson, we hope learners will:

- ⚲ Recognize how data can be manipulated or presented in ways that trigger emotional responses
- ⚲ Consider their responsibility in applying strategies for parsing credibility to data

Curricula Connections

Target Audience	9th–12th (As with all lessons in this book, this grade span is a suggestion only. With a few adaptations, this lesson could easily be applied to other learners.)

Potential Content Area Connections/Collaborations

- Health: Conception, child rearing
- Sociology/Psychology: Grouping, rites of passage, motivations for making pacts
- History: Militarism, origin of West Point

ISTE Standards

Students

- Knowledge Constructor (3b): Students evaluate the accuracy, perspective, credibility and relevance of information, media, data or other resources.
- Knowledge Constructor (3d): Students build knowledge by actively exploring real-world issues and problems, developing ideas and theories and pursuing answers and solutions.
- Computational Thinker (5c): Students break problems into component parts, extract key information, and develop descriptive models to understand complex systems or facilitate problem-solving.

Educators

- Citizen (3b): Educators establish a learning culture that promotes curiosity and critical examination of online resources and fosters digital literacy and media fluency.
- Designer (5b): Educators design authentic learning activities that align with content area standards and use digital tools and resources to maximize active, deep learning.
- Facilitator (6b): Educators manage technology and student learning strategies in digital platforms, virtual environments, hands-on makerspaces or in the field.
- Analyst (7a): Educators provide alternative ways for students to demonstrate competency and reflect on their learning using technology.

Learning Objectives

By the end of this lesson:

- The learner will apply the Four Lenses to information as a step in determining credibility.
- The learner will understand how data can be manipulated to influence.
- The learner will evaluate several resources for evidence of data manipulation.
- The learner will classify a variety of data according to their credibility red flags.
- The learner will synthesize learning by creating an interactive image to share specific data set analysis.

Resources Needed for This Lesson

Reminder: A variety of resources related to this chapter can be found in the Digital Detective's Evidence Locker. Use the QR code to the left, or visit evidencelocker.online. Then navigate to Chapter 10.

Time Needed for This Lesson: 2–4 hours

Case File

The following supplemental resources from the Digital Detective's Evidence Locker may be given to students to examine the case. Be sure to note which resources for this story reveal the facts of the case.

- [IMAGE] Hi-res version of the image shared in the student one-sheet
- [VIDEO] Annual West Point Pillow Fight Gone Wild
- [GRAPH] West Point Data Drama
- [ARTICLE] Teens May Have Made Pact to Get Pregnant
- [ARTICLE] At West Point, Annual Pillow Fight Becomes Weaponized

Process

1. Activating Prior Knowledge/Hook:

☑ Step/Tasks

a. Review the Four Lenses (see Chapters 1–4).
b. Have students share what they know about emotional triggers.
c. Red herrings, or false clues, are an important component of this lesson. You may wish to review what they are with students.

Suggested Resources

For this step, check in the Digital Detective's Evidence Locker for:

- [VIDEO] Red Herrings

2. Guided Practice Part 1: The Initial Hypothesis

✅ Step/Tasks

a. Working individually (or in pairs), have students review the one-sheet for The Case of . . . The Pillow Fight Pact!
b. Students should record and classify clues related to the Four Lenses as they review the case.
   - ▶ Note: If you're using a traditional information literacy protocol (see Chapter 3) with students, now is the time to refer to it. However, remember that we recommend that these only be used as jumping-off points for learners: kindling to help spark their own investigations.
c. Product: By the end of this part of the lesson, student detective teams should generate an initial hypothesis, or theory of the case.
d. Optional: Have students share their initial hypothesis with the group.

Suggested Resources

For this step, check in the Digital Detective's Evidence Locker for:

- [TEMPLATE] Evidence Log (a tool that may support students as they detect and document clues from the case)
- [TEMPLATE] Case Synopsis (a tool that may support students as they present their final verdicts in the case)

3. Guided Practice Part 2: The Case File

✅ Step/Tasks

a. Give students access to selected items from the case file, noting that some of these items reveal the facts of the case.
b. Using a digital tool like Mentimeter, have students vote on which piece of evidence from the case file was the most convincing to them.
   - ▶ For an added layer of complexity, have students rank each item from the case file in terms of which they would be most likely to cite if they were assigned a research paper on West Point (which would include information about the Pillow Fight).

⊚ **Suggested Resources**

For this step, check in the Digital Detective's Evidence Locker for:

- [VIDEO] Tutorial for Mentimeter

4. Assessment

☑ **Step/Tasks**

At this point, students should be ready to deliver a verdict on the case.

a. Individually, have students report their findings, including their final verdict regarding the story's credibility. Student responses can be recorded using the Case Synopsis template from the Digital Detective's Notebook or through a digital voting tool, such as Kahoot!, Poll Everywhere, or Socrative.

⊚ **Suggested Resources**

For this step, check in the Digital Detective's Evidence Locker for:

- [TEMPLATE] Case Synopsis

5. Whole Group Debrief

☑ **Step/Tasks**

a. Together, as a whole group, have students debate the various theories of the case.
b. Individually or as a group, have students rate their own confidence in their verdict of the case.
  ▶ We recommend using a Likert Scale for capturing this information. Digital tools such as Google Forms and Mentimeter are great options for creating this scale.

⊚ **Suggested Resources**

For this step, check in the Digital Detective's Evidence Locker for:

- [VIDEO] How to Use Likert Scales

6. Solution: Reveal the Facts of the Case! (See Below!)

☑ **Step/Tasks**

a. It's time to let students know where this story fell on the credibility spectrum. To do this, use the document The Facts of the Case (see the following section) to reveal the evidence associated with each lens that students should have uncovered.
b. We recommend that you also provide students with the opportunity to add evidence to the facts of the case. Students may have found other clues under each lens that can help their classmates think more deeply about credibility detection.

7. Synthesis

☑ Step/Tasks

To help students synthesize their learning, we want them to think more deeply about how data can be used to manipulate and influence people.

a. Have students watch either/both videos on data evaluation.

b. Then have students list different data points that were shared either in the one-sheet or the case file.

c. Using the infographic When the Numbers Don't Add Up and the article "When Bars Face Down," have students classify the examples they cited into different categories.

d. Then, using a tool like ThingLink, Genially, or Google Slides, have students create an interactive image featuring the image West Point Data Drama (from the case file) in which they tag, label, and analyze every credibility red flag that they spot in the graphic. (Note: They should be able to identify at least one of every example from the When the Numbers Don't Add Up infographic.) Their analysis should include both what type of red flag they spotted and why it negatively affects credibility.

  ▶ Note: It may help students to view the raw West Point enrollment/graduation data (which is also in the case file). Comparing both data sets may help students spot credibility red flags in the image.

◉ Suggested Resources

For this step, check in the Digital Detective's Evidence Locker for links to:

- [VIDEO] Trusting the Numbers—Tips for Analyzing Data
- [VIDEO] Crash Course—Tips for Analyzing Data and Infographics
- [ARTICLE] When Bars Face Down
- [SPREADSHEET] West Point 1980–2018 Graduation and Commissioning Rates
- [INFOGRAPHIC] When the Numbers Don't Add Up
- [VIDEO] Tutorial for ThingLink
- [VIDEO] Tutorial for Genially

8. Reflection

☑ Step/Tasks

a. As a final tag on their interactive image, we recommend having students complete the What's My Job? reflection. For this tag, have students write or record answers to the following questions:

  ▶ Now that I understand how data can be manipulated to influence me, what is my job? What are some specific habits I need to develop in order to ensure that I don't trust or spread manipulated data?

9. Scaffolds

Chapters 3 and 4 offer mini-lessons that may be helpful as scaffolds for this unit.

- Heads Up Game—Version 2 (Chapter 4, Motives)
- What Makes a Good Question Meme? (Chapter 3, Forensics)
- Mis Dis or Mal Information—Matching Game (Chapter 4, Motives)

10. Potential Extensions

- Using a data set of their choosing and the resources from this lesson, have students create a misleading infographic. To add an extra layer of complexity, have them also create a nefarious person who will act as the infographic creator. This persona should include the specific motivations of the individual who is manipulating the data to further an agenda. Be sure to check in the evidence locker for resources to help create infographics and a website that archives misleading correlations.

Verdict **RED** | **FALSE** [Do Not Share]

Lens

LENS 1: TRIGGERS

Clues related to how elements of the story are designed to elicit, or trigger, an extreme emotional response.

Evidence

- Although not the primary lens through which this story should be analyzed, the Triggers Lens plays an important role in recognizing the importance of data analysis/evaluation. The overemphasis of certain data points (or the hiding of others) may be strategies for triggering an emotional response. If emphasized numbers elicit emotions such as fear or anger, this must be identified as a credibility red flag.

Lens

LENS 2: ACCESS

Clues related to the device upon which the story is being viewed and how that access might change the way a Digital Detective locates evidence.

Evidence

- Although not the primary lens through which this story is viewed, Access does play a role in determining credibility. Apps like YouTube include details such as likes and share counts, which may affect our urge to trust or share information.
- Additionally, YouTube prioritizes comments based on user profiles. Information consumers must take extra steps to sort comments by date posted.

LENS 3: FORENSICS

Clues found in the details of the story, including (but not limited to) the URL, date published, authorship, and authority.

Evidence

- Forensics is the most relevant lens through which to view this story. Credibility red flags related to the data contained throughout the case file provide the most compelling evidence. Through their investigation, students should spot all of the following:
  - ▶ Misaligned data: Student enrollments are compared to graduation rates.
  - ▶ Overemphasis of data: The difference between the number of students enrolled and the number of cadets who graduated is emphasized.
  - ▶ Confusing graphs: The graph depicting enrollment and graduation rates is presented upside down.
  - ▶ Red herrings: Numerous red herrings exist throughout the case file. From the number of students accepted to West Point each year to information about pregnancy pacts, this superfluous information exists only to distract.
- While lateral reading will quickly reveal that a violent turn at the annual pillow fight did result in the tradition being ended, there is no evidence to suggest that it was related to enrollment data or a misguided pregnancy pact.

LENS 4: MOTIVES

Clues found in the motivations of potential suspects and how the story is created, shared, etc.

Evidence

- While the Motives Lens is not the primary one through which students should view this case, the motives of individuals who manipulate data to further an agenda are important to discuss.
- **Lineup:** If you choose to do a lineup activity for this lesson, we suggest the following suspects: The Concerned Cousin, The Grifter, **The Blue Liar**, and The Scaremonger. Although we created this lesson with The Blue Liar in mind, students will likely be able to create compelling arguments for all the suspects in the suggested lineup. Remember, there's no one right answer; rather, the goal is for Digital Detectives to recognize that the information shouldn't be shared or trusted.

The case of . . . **The Bogus Burrito!**

The Scene

They say all publicity is good publicity, but pop star Justin Bieber might disagree. Paparazzi recently caught the musician in what has turned out to be a compromising position! Redditors were disturbed by this photo of Bieber eating a burrito most unusually!

The image was quickly transformed into countless memes, many questioning whether Bieber had suffered some kind of mental breakdown. Comments like "He looks like someone who has never seen a burrito!" and "This is what happens when we hand out burritos without instruction manuals" received hundreds of thousands of likes as the photo went viral.

At a time when many celebrities are struggling to earn money, this hit to Bieber's image could result in long-term damage to the singer's reputation.

Possible Clues (Questions to Think About)

- **Triggers:** How does this information make you feel about the people involved? Does that play a role in making you want to like/share it?
- **Access:** Does the app being used make it easier or more difficult to determine credibility?
- **Forensics:** Are there clues in the information itself that can help to determine credibility?
- **Motives:** If this story turns out to be fake, what kind of person would create/spread it?

Is this story about a burrito brunch gone wrong, or is there nothing to taco 'bout here?

💡 Big Ideas

This lesson focuses on the *Motives* and *Forensics* Lenses. In 2019, a *New York Times* article titled "Nazi Symbols and Racist Memes: Combating School Intolerance" (MacFarquhar) about how memes are used to recruit young white males to white supremacy groups caught the attention of many educators. Shortly after that, Stanford University historian and researcher Sam Wineburg used Twitter to trace a meme's journey to spread racist propaganda (2019). His analysis of how such memes play on emotions, perhaps most among readers who lack a basic understanding of history, was both fascinating and frightening. This analysis, coupled with a recent study from Project Information Literacy focusing on college students' news habits, revealed interesting trends, including that memes are a common and trusted source of information for young people (Denton, 2018). Digital Detectives must understand how to analyze and evaluate these bite-sized, ubiquitous portals of information. The objectives below have been designed to help learners think deeply about the motivations of people who make memes and the significant consequences these small packages can deliver.

🖌️ SEL Spotlight

Memes are easy to share, often disguised as jokes, and have become popular ways to communicate with others. According to a 2016 study from the Center for Peace Studies and Violence Prevention at Virginia Tech, the number of Americans between the ages of 15 and 21 who reported seeing extremist content online jumped by about 20 percent, to 70.2 percent from 58.3 percent, between 2013 and 2016 (Fifer, 2017). It's no surprise that memes have also become a popular vehicle for delivering this content to young people. Through these activities, we encourage learners to:

- Explore how small information packages of information can trigger significant emotional reactions
- Recognize that memes are both generated by and about real people who are often affected in profound ways when they go viral

♀ Think about their responsibility in sharing memes that lack consideration for the people involved

Curricula Connections

Target Audience	9th–12th (As with all lessons in this book, this grade span is a suggestion only. With a few adaptations, this lesson could easily be applied to other learners.)

Potential Content Area Connections/Collaborations

- ELA: Finding motive, developing ideas and theories, the research process, understanding puns
- Science: Building a hypothesis, the research process, how a process works
- History: Propaganda
- Psychology: Human motivations, social constructivism, constructivism

ISTE Standards

Students

- Knowledge Constructor (3b): Students evaluate the accuracy, perspective, credibility and relevance of information, media, data or other resources.
- Knowledge Constructor (3d): Students build knowledge by actively exploring real-world issues and problems, developing ideas and theories and pursuing answers and solutions.
- Computational Thinker (5c): Students break problems into component parts, extract key information, and develop descriptive models to understand complex systems or facilitate problem-solving.
- Creative Communicator (5c): Students communicate complex ideas clearly and effectively by creating or using various digital objects such as visualizations, models or simulations.

Educators

- Citizen (3b): Educators establish a learning culture that promotes curiosity and critical examination of online resources and fosters digital literacy and media fluency.
- Designer (5b): Educators design authentic learning activities that align with content area standards and use digital tools and resources to maximize active, deep learning.
- Facilitator (6b): Educators manage the use of technology and student learning strategies in digital platforms, virtual environments, hands-on makerspaces or in the field.

Learning Objectives

By the end of this lesson:

- The learner will apply the Four Lenses to information as a step in determining credibility.
- The learner will examine the art of memes and how they might influence people.
- The learner will compare and contrast the motives for creating and sharing memes.
- The learner will work with classmates to synthesize the facts of the case.
- The learner will synthesize learning by creating a meme.

Resources Needed for This Lesson

Reminder: A variety of resources related to this chapter can be found in the Digital Detective's Evidence Locker. Use the QR code to the left, or visit evidencelocker.online. Then navigate to Chapter 10.

Time Needed for This Lesson: 2–4 hours

Case File

The following supplemental resources from the Digital Detective's Evidence Locker may be given to students to examine the case. Be sure to note which resources for this story reveal the facts of the case.

- [IMAGE] Hi-res version of the image shared in the student one-sheet.
- [ARTICLE] Does Justin Bieber Know How to Eat a Burrito?
- [VIDEO] Does Justin Bieber Not Know How Burritos Work?
- [VIDEO] Memes That Ruined Lives
- [ARTICLE] "Justin Bieber's Burrito" and Other Foods Eaten "Wrong"

Process

1. Activating Prior Knowledge/Hook:

☑ Step/Tasks

a. Review the Four Lenses (see Chapters 1–4).
b. Have students share what they know about memes.
  ▸ Using a collaborative tool like Padlet, have students share a link to a meme representing how they feel about the school year so far.

⊚ Suggested Resources

For this step, check in the Digital Detective's Evidence Locker for:

- [VIDEO] Tutorial for Padlet

2. Guided Practice Part 1: The Initial Hypothesis

☑ Step/Tasks

a. Working individually (or in pairs), have students review the one-sheet for The Case of . . . The Bogus Burrito!
b. Students should record and classify clues related to the Four Lenses as they review the case.
  ▶ Note: If you're using a traditional information literacy protocol (see Chapter 3) with students, now is the time to refer to it. However, remember that we recommend that these only be used as jumping-off points for learners: kindling to help spark their own investigations.
c. Product: By the end of this part of the lesson, student detective teams should generate an initial hypothesis or theory of the case.
d. Optional: Have students share their initial hypothesis with the group.

⊚ Suggested Resources

For this step, check in the Digital Detective's Evidence Locker for:

- [TEMPLATE] Evidence Log (a tool that may support students as they detect and document clues from the case)
- [TEMPLATE] Case Synopsis (a tool that may support students as they present their final verdicts in the case)

3. Guided Practice Part 2: The Case File

☑ Step/Tasks

a. Give students access to selected items from the case file, noting that some of these items reveal the facts of the case.
b. After reviewing the case file, have students play the game Memeland in small groups.
  ▶ While playing, have students record the various motivations that are presented for creating and sharing a meme.
  ▶ For an added layer of complexity, have them match each motive with a potential suspect from Chapter 2.
c. When finished, have students discuss which examples from the game they disagreed with or that could have represented multiple motives.
d. Finally, have students identify the motive for creating the Bieber Burrito meme, noting that those motives will likely differ depending on whether the meme turns out to be real or fake.

🔘 Suggested Resources

For this step, check in the Digital Detective's Evidence Locker for:

- [VIDEO] Tutorial for Mentimeter
- [GAME] Memeland

4. Assessment

☑️ Step/Tasks

At this point, students should be ready to deliver a verdict on the case.

a. Individually, have students report their findings, including their final verdict regarding the story's credibility. Student responses can be recorded using the Case Synopsis template from the Digital Detective's Notebook or through a digital voting tool, such as Kahoot!, Poll Everywhere, or Socrative.

🔘 Suggested Resources

For this step, check in the Digital Detective's Evidence Locker for:

- [TEMPLATE] Case Synopsis

5. Whole Group Debrief

☑️ Step/Tasks

a. Together, as a whole group, have students debate the various theories of the case.
b. Individually or as a group, have students rate their own confidence in their verdicts.
   ▶ We recommend using a Likert Scale for capturing this information. Digital tools such as Google Forms and Mentimeter are great options for creating this scale.

🔘 Suggested Resources

For this step, check in the Digital Detective's Evidence Locker for:

- [VIDEO] How to Use Likert Scales

6. Solution: Reveal the Facts of the Case! (See Below!)

☑️ Step/Tasks

a. At this point, it's time to let students know where this story fell on the credibility spectrum. Use the document The Facts of the Case (see the following section) to reveal the evidence associated with each lens that students should have uncovered.
b. We recommend that you also provide students with the opportunity to add evidence to the facts of the case. Students may have found other clues under each lens that can help their classmates think more deeply about credibility detection.

7. Synthesis

☑ Step/Tasks

To help students synthesize their learning, we want them to think more deeply about how/ why memes are created. Have students choose from the following options to demonstrate their understanding.

- Option 1: For this option, students will need to use the curated list of memes they created at the beginning of this lesson and the infographic Memeland (which is a supplement to the game they played earlier). Using these two resources, first have students identify frequently used design choices in the memes they curated as a class. Do they see the use of all caps or bold text, single-block coloring or excessive punctuation repeated throughout these examples? Have them make a list of the design elements they see most often. Then have students "vote up" the most effective memes from this activity, which will give them a list of the top 10 (or so) best memes as voted on by the class. Finally, have students compare those memes to the list of design strategies they identified earlier. What do they notice about specific design elements that seem to result in a more significant impact/ influence?
- Option 2: Using a randomizer tool such as Name Picker Ninja, randomly assign students both a celebrity and a potential suspect. Using a digital tool such as those in the Tools for Making Your Own Memes resource collection, have students create a meme about their assigned celebrity from the perspective of their assigned suspect. Then have students share their memes, explaining their design choices.
- Option 3: If you've allowed students to choose from Options 1 and 2, have both groups analyze the completed memes' design effectiveness. Using the information curated from those students who completed the Option 1 activity, have students rank which of the memes created by those students who completed Option 2 would likely be most effective.

🔘 Suggested Resources

For this step, check in the Digital Detective's Evidence Locker for:

- [VIDEO] Tutorial for Padlet
- [RESOURCE COLLECTION] Tools for Making Your Own Memes
- [INFOGRAPHIC] Memeland
- [VIDEO] Tutorial for Meme Generators

8. Reflection

☑ **Step/Tasks**

a. For this lesson, we recommend using a tool like Flipgrid to allow students to reflect on their work with a discussion prompt. Here is a list of potential discussion topics:

   ▶ Do celebrities deserve to be targets of memes? Would you feel differently about the burrito meme if it had featured someone who wasn't famous?

   ▶ Memes have become popular tools for white supremacist groups sharing propaganda. Considering what you learned from this lesson, why do you think extremist groups prefer this type of communication?

   ▶ What's one way you can change your behavior to help other people (not in this class) think more critically about memes?

9. Scaffolds

Chapters 1 and 3 offer mini-lessons that may be helpful as scaffolds for this unit.

- Information Literacy Likert Scale/Mood Meter (Chapter 1, Triggers)
- Speed or Brake Activity (Chapter 1, Triggers)
- What Makes a Good Question Meme? (Chapter 3, Forensic)

10. Potential Extensions

- Using the infographic It's Your Move (located in the Digital Detective's Evidence Locker), have students create memes that trigger one of the Big Seven emotions that are most used by marketers to trigger consumer responses. Then have students identify a list of suspects (from Chapter 4) who would be most motivated to create a meme triggering each specific emotion.

Verdict **RED** | **FALSE** [Do Not Share]

Lens

LENS 1: TRIGGERS

Clues related to how elements of the story are designed to elicit, or trigger, an extreme emotional response.

Evidence

- Although the Triggers Lens is not the primary one through which this story should be analyzed, triggers do play an important role in thinking about why memes are useful for communicating information. In this case, students may feel superior to Justin Bieber or feel sorry for him. Either way, they need to understand how these emotions may affect their work as Digital Detectives.

Lens

LENS 2: ACCESS

Clues related to the device upon which the story is being viewed and how that access might change the way a Digital Detective locates evidence.

Evidence

- Although not the primary lens through which this story is viewed, Access does play a role in determining credibility. Apps such as Reddit make it challenging to trace information back to its original source. Digital Detectives must be mindful that the person sharing the information may not be the person who created it.
- Reddit is also unique in that it posts both user and thread IDs next to one another. In this case, the thread ID, r/things4PHDs, may affect whether students see the user as more or less credible. However, threads in Reddit are created and named by autonomous users.
- Additionally, Reddit prioritizes comments based on voting trends. Information consumers must take extra steps to sort comments by date posted.

Lens

LENS 3: FORENSICS

Clues found in the details of the story, including (but not limited to) the URL, date published, authorship, and authority.

Evidence

- Forensics is an essential lens through which Digital Detectives should approach this case. A lack of information about who initially took this photo and no comment from the subject of the photo are both credibility red flags.
- The photo itself should be suspicious, as we cannot see Bieber's face.
- Digital Detectives may also notice that the story in the case file was written by a food reporter (whose expertise does not seem to extend to celebrities).
- Finally, the use of all-caps text, such as *CAN SOMEONE PLEASE CHECK ON THE BIEBS??* in the photo, should be a clue that this story may be more sensational than factual.

Lens

LENS 4: MOTIVES

Clues found in the motivations of potential suspects and how the story is created, shared, etc.

Evidence

- The Motives Lens is the primary lens through which this story should be viewed. Although we want Digital Detectives to consider specific suspects who may be responsible for creating this story, the bigger picture involves them thinking about how memes, in particular, can be used to mislead and influence.
- **Lineup:** If you choose to do a lineup activity for this lesson, we suggest the following suspects: The Doppelgänger, The Stan, The Wannabe, and The Jokester. This case provides an example of **The Hydra**, a bonus suspect in which the characteristics of several suspects are adopted. While we created this with all of the suspects in our lineup as potential components of The Hydra, students may have compelling arguments for including still others. Remember, there's no one right answer; rather, the goal is for Digital Detectives to recognize that the information shouldn't be shared or trusted.

The Case of . . . **The This Is Your New Teacher Challenge!**

The Scene

Although this back-to-school "challenge" began on TikTok, videos like these are now being posted everywhere! The idea is simple; record your child's reaction when shown a photo of their new teacher. There's just one catch . . . the goal is to make sure the picture is so scary that the child bursts into tears!

Unbelievably, parents are trolling the internet for photos of people whose physical appearance is likely to shock or upset their children so that they can record and share this trauma with followers. To make the practice even more disturbing, the photos being chosen are often of people with physical disabilities.

What started as a joke has turned into a viral opportunity to upset young kids and bully vulnerable people online.

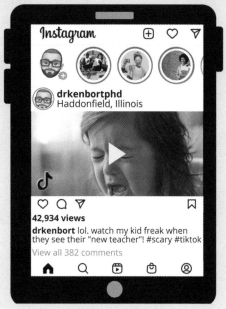

Possible Clues (Questions to Think About)

- **Triggers:** How does this information make you feel about the people involved? Does that play a role in making you want to like/share it?
- **Access:** How does cross-posting between apps affect your ability to trace the original source?
- **Forensics:** Are there clues in the information itself that can help us determine credibility?
- **Motives:** If this story turns out to be true, who are the intended and unintended victims?

Is this example of pitiful parenting true?

💡 Big Ideas

This lesson focuses on the *Triggers* and *Access* Lenses. We've all heard the expression "too good to be true." But what happens when a story is too *horrible* to be true? This story's adults' behavior may cause some students to automatically dismiss it as being too incredible or outrageous to be real. Additionally, the revelation that it is true may cause them to question parents' trustworthiness (or adults) as a group. As we've explored in previous chapters, the information we consume not only helps to shape our identities and how we view ourselves but also plays a role in shaping how we view others. Additionally, the "group think" of internet challenges like this one, coupled with the ease of passing along information that triggers a strong emotion (provided by the Community Reading Experience), can be powerful influencers. The objectives below have been designed to help learners think deeply about how social media and the apps we use to engage with our communities influence behavior and tempt us to engage in activities we might otherwise find abhorrent on our own.

🐝 SEL Spotlight

Seeing a photograph of someone whose physical appearance challenges social norms is often not enough to keep us from comparing the individual in the image to widely accepted standards of beauty. However, when we learn more about the person in the photo, it becomes more difficult to judge them harshly. As children's author Kate DiCamillo famously said, "Stories connect us." When we know a person's story, we're more likely to empathize with them and engage in behavior driven by what we have in common with that person instead of focusing on the things that divide us. Many of the apps we use to share and consume information are image- or short video–driven. While this may make it easier for us to connect the content to a strong emotional response, connecting those responses to the story behind the image requires more work. Through these activities, we encourage learners to:

- 📍 Explore how emotional triggers influence our urge to join internet challenges and other viral bandwagons

- Recognize how content that pushes us to judge other people also serves to shape our own identities
- Consider how being the subject of viral content can impact the identities of those who may be unwilling participants
- Reflect on how their participation in viral challenges may affect their credibility as a source of information or online community member
- Understand the various aspects (e.g., moral, social, emotional, or practical) of challenging situations

Curricula Connections

Target Audience	9th–12th (As with all lessons in this book, this grade span is a suggestion only. With a few adaptations, this lesson could easily be applied to other learners.)

Potential Content Area Connections/Collaborations

- ELA: Point of view
- Health: Psychosocial, individual, family, and social recovery
- Science: Causes of physical disabilities, whether hereditary, congenital, or induced by birth or trauma
- Sociology: Group dynamics, group think
- Psychology: Bullying, emotional distress, and anxiety

ISTE Standards

Students

- Knowledge Constructor (3b): Students evaluate the accuracy, perspective, credibility and relevance of information, media, data or other resources.
- Knowledge Constructor (3d): Students build knowledge by actively exploring real-world issues and problems, developing ideas and theories and pursuing answers and solutions.
- Computational Thinker (5c): Students break problems into component parts, extract key information, and develop descriptive models to understand complex systems or facilitate problem-solving.

Educators

- Citizen (3b): Educators establish a learning culture that promotes curiosity and critical examination of online resources and fosters digital literacy and media fluency.
- Designer (5b): Educators design authentic learning activities that align with content area standards and use digital tools and resources to maximize active, deep learning.
- Facilitator (6b): Educators manage the use of technology and student learning strategies in digital platforms, virtual environments, hands-on makerspaces or in the field.
- Analyst (7a): Educators provide alternative ways for students to demonstrate competency and reflect on their learning using technology.

Learning Objectives

By the end of this lesson:

- The learner will apply the Four Lenses to information as a step in determining credibility.
- The learner will explore how the Community Reading Experience exploits group think to promote viral challenges.
- The learner will use written conversations to analyze how social media often amplifies content without meaningful context.
- The learner will synthesize learning by considering how point of view affects Digital Detective work.
- The learner will reflect on how participating in digital challenges affects the credibility of content creators.

Resources Needed for This Lesson

Reminder: A variety of resources related to this chapter can be found in the Digital Detective's Evidence Locker. Use the QR code to the left, or visit evidencelocker.online. Then navigate to Chapter 10.

Time Needed for This Lesson: 2–4 hours

Case File

The following supplemental resources from the Digital Detective's Evidence Locker may be given to students to examine the case. Be sure to note which resources for this story reveal the facts of the case.

- [IMAGE] Hi-res version of the image shared in the student one-sheet
- [INSTAGRAM POST] I knew it was coming: The New Teacher Challenge featuring ME
- [VIDEO] New Teacher Challenge Video Compilation
- [ARTICLE] The #NewTeacherChallenge Is HILARIOUS!
- [ARTICLE] The Social Media Challenges Helping Keep Boredom at Bay
- [ARTICLE] The Danger of Internet Challenges

Process

1. Activating Prior Knowledge/Hook:

☑ Step/Tasks

a. Review the Four Lenses (see Chapters 1–4).
b. Have students brainstorm what they know about viral internet challenges. They might be familiar with the Ice Bucket or Mannequin Challenges.
c. Using a tool like Dotstorming, have students brainstorm why they think people get involved with those challenges. Then have them "vote up" the causes they believe are most likely.

◉ Suggested Resources

For this step, check in the Digital Detective's Evidence Locker for:

- [VIDEO] Tutorial for Using the Tool Dotstorming

2. Guided Practice Part 1: The Initial Hypothesis

☑ Step/Tasks

a. Working individually (or in pairs), have students review the one-sheet for The Case of . . . The This Is Your New Teacher Challenge!
b. Students should record and classify clues related to the Four Lenses as they review the case.
   ▶ Note: If you're using a traditional information literacy protocol (see Chapter 3) with students, now is the time to refer to it. However, remember that we recommend that these only be used as jumping-off points for learners: kindling to help spark their own investigations.
c. Product: By the end of this part of the lesson, student detective teams should generate an initial hypothesis or theory of the case.
d. Optional: Have students share their initial hypothesis with the group.

⟳ Suggested Resources

For this step, check in the Digital Detective's Evidence Locker for:

- [TEMPLATE] Evidence Log (a tool that may support students as they detect and document clues from the case)
- [TEMPLATE] Case Synopsis (a tool that may support students as they present their final verdicts in the case)

3. Guided Practice Part 2: The Case File

☑ Step/Tasks

a. Give students access to selected items from the case file, noting that some of these items reveal the facts of the case.
b. After reviewing the case file, in small groups, have students use a digital tool such as Padlet or Google Slides to have a written conversation about how the Community Reading Experience contributes to the popularity of internet challenges like the one described in this case.

⟳ Suggested Resources

For this step, check in the Digital Detective's Evidence Locker for:

- [INFOGRAPHIC] What's Not to Like?
- [EXEMPLAR] Written Conversation

4. Assessment

☑ Step/Tasks

At this point, students should be ready to deliver a verdict on the case.

a. Individually, have students report their findings, including their final verdict regarding the story's credibility. Student responses can be recorded using the Case Synopsis template from the Digital Detective's Notebook or through a digital voting tool, such as Kahoot!, Poll Everywhere, or Socrative.

⟳ Suggested Resources

For this step, check in the Digital Detective's Evidence Locker for:

- [TEMPLATE] Case Synopsis

5. Whole Group Debrief

☑ Step/Tasks

a. Together, as a whole group, have students debate the various theories of the case.

b. Individually or as a group, have students rate their confidence in their verdicts of the case.
   - ▶ We recommend using a Likert Scale for capturing this information. Digital tools such as Google Forms and Mentimeter are great options for creating this scale.

◉ Suggested Resources

For this step, check in the Digital Detective's Evidence Locker for:

- [VIDEO] How to Use Likert Scales

6. Solution: Reveal the Facts of the Case! (See Below!)

☑ Step/Tasks

a. At this point, it's time to let students know where this story fell on the credibility spectrum. To do this, use the document The Facts of the Case (see the following section) to reveal the evidence associated with each lens that students should have uncovered.

b. We recommend that you also provide students with the opportunity to add evidence to the facts of the case. Students may have found other clues under each lens that can help their classmates think more deeply about credibility detection.

7. Synthesis

☑ Step/Tasks

To help students synthesize their learning, we want them to think more deeply about how participation in viral internet challenges can affect how we view others and how others view us. To do this, divide students into three groups in which they each tell the story of the This Is Your New Teacher Challenge from a different perspective using a tool such as Book Creator, Adobe Spark, or other digital storytelling tool.

- Group 1: Tell the story from the perspective of the parent who, years in the future, must share why and how they chose to participate in the challenge. Parents' stories should include details about:
  - ▶ How/where they first heard about the challenge
  - ▶ What convinced them to participate
  - ▶ What steps they took to create their video
  - ▶ How they felt at the time of the challenge
  - ▶ How they feel now that they know the emotional consequences of the challenge

- Group 2: Tell the story from the perspective of the (now grown) child whose parent pranked them by posting a #newteacherchallenge video to social media. Childrens' stories should include details about:
  - ▶ How they remember feeling at the time they were pranked
  - ▶ How the prank affected their parent's credibility as a member of the online community
  - ▶ What questions they would like to ask their parent about their participation in the challenge
  - ▶ What they would say to the person whose picture was used as the example of a "scary" teacher
- Group 3: Tell the story from the perspective of the person whose picture was used as the example of the "scary" teacher in the challenge. These accounts should include details about:
  - ▶ How it feels to have your image used in this way
  - ▶ What they would say to parents who are tempted to participate in these challenges
  - ▶ What they wish the kids who were pranked knew about them as a person
- Then combine the stories into one product that can be shared. For an extra layer of complexity, have students record their reflections (see below) and add them to the combined book's end.

🔘 Suggested Resources

For this step, check in the Digital Detective's Evidence Locker for links to:

a. [VIDEO] Book Creator Tutorial
b. [VIDEO] Adobe Spark Tutorial
c. [VIDEO] Tutorial for Digital Audio File Recording

8. Reflection

☑ Step/Tasks

a. For this activity, we recommend the "First I thought_____, but now I think _____" reflection. Either in writing or as an audio/video addition to the synthesis activity, have students complete a "First I thought_____, but now I think _____" reflection (for each of the perspectives represented above). Then have them explore how their opinion of each person involved changed as they learned more about the challenge and how social media played a role in their participation in it.

9. Scaffolds

Chapters 1 and 2 offer mini-lessons that may be helpful as scaffolds for this unit.

- Finish This Comic! 2 (Chapter 1, Triggers)
- Information Literacy Identity Webs (Chapter 1, Triggers)
- Community Reading Experience TAKE 2 (Chapter 2, Access)

10. Potential Extensions

- Using the graphic novel *When Stars Are Scattered* by Victoria Jamieson and Omar Mohamed, have students create a one-sheet in which they use only part of Omar's story to influence action (either positive or negative) related to the central issue of the story: the refugee experience. You'll find a video trailer for *When Stars Are Scattered* in the Digital Detective's Evidence Locker. Note: Other books can be used to achieve this task. The key to the selection process will be the idea that when only part of a story is told, it's easier to manipulate opinion about it.

THE FACTS OF THE CASE

Verdict **GREEN** | **TRUE** [Share with Credit]

Lens

LENS 1: TRIGGERS

Clues related to how elements of the story are designed to elicit, or trigger, an extreme emotional response.

Evidence

- The Triggers Lens is a critical one through which Digital Detectives should view this story. In addition to how the images in the videos shared through the case file may trigger strong emotions, it's crucial for learners to also think about how challenges like this trigger:
  - ▶ A desire to belong and participate
  - ▶ A feeling of superiority toward the individuals depicted as "scary"
  - ▶ Questions about the people who participated in the challenge—in this case, parents!

Lens

LENS 2: ACCESS

Clues related to the device upon which the story is being viewed and how that access might change the way a Digital Detective locates evidence.

Evidence

- Access is another crucial lens that Digital Detectives should consider when analyzing this story.
- By taking a minute to consider the potential consequences of participating in the #newteacherchallenge, most people would likely decide not to join in. Digital Detectives need to recognize that social media apps like TikTok, Instagram, and the like are designed to encourage our participation by making it easy to like/share and promote the positive reinforcement of other people liking/sharing our posts.
- Additionally, although not critical to determining credibility in this case, it may be meaningful to discuss how apps like TikTok allow for cross-posting, adding to the layers of complexity Digital Detectives face when attempting to triangulate a primary source.
- Finally, hashtags like #newteacherchallenge make it very easy for us to participate in community experiences without considering the other members. This story allows Digital Detectives to think about how hashtags can be used as metadata (allowing us to search for content) and value statements (allowing us to signal what matters most about the information being shared).

Lens

LENS 3: FORENSICS

Clues found in the details of the story, including (but not limited to) the URL, date published, authorship, and authority.

Evidence

- Suppose you are using a credibility protocol, such as the CRAAP Test or SIFT model, with your students. If you are, this case provides an excellent opportunity to explore how the concept of authority applies to groups and individual sources. In this case, none of the respective sources possess any markers of credibility. Still, their identification as parents may be influential to Digital Detectives, who may assume that, as a group, parents can be trusted.

Lens

LENS 4: MOTIVES

Clues found in the motivations of potential suspects and how the story is created, shared, etc.

Evidence

- Although not the primary lens through which this story should be viewed, this case provides Digital Detectives with an opportunity to consider how motivations differ from values. For example:
  ▶ While showing kindness toward others is a value many hold, the motivation to belong or be a part of a global phenomenon may overshadow that value.
- **Lineup:** If you choose to do a lineup activity for this lesson, we suggest the following suspects: The Lemming, The Wannabe, The Outsider, and The Cyborg. Because this story is true, the correct answer will be **None of the Above**. However, students may make compelling arguments for any of these suspects.

References

Adams, J. (n.d.). *Adams' argument for the defense: 3–4 December 1770*. Founders Online, National Archives. https://founders.archives.gov/documents/Adams/05-03-02-0001-0004-0016

Adichie, C. N. (2009, July). *The danger of a single story* [Video]. TED Conferences. https://www.ted.com/talks/chimamanda_ngozi_adichie_the_danger_of_a_single_story?language=en

Allyn, B. (2020, June 16). *Study exposes Russia disinformation campaign that operated in the shadows for 6 years*. NPR. https://www.npr.org/2020/06/16/878169027/study-exposes-russia-disinformation-campaign-that-operated-in-the-shadows-for-6-

Anderson, J., & Rainie, L. (2017, October 19). *The future of truth and misinformation online*. Pew Research Center. https://www.pewresearch.org/internet/2017/10/19/the-future-of-truth-and-misinformation-online

Anderson, M., & Jiang, J. (2018, May 31). *Teens, social media & technology 2018*. Pew Research Center. https://www.pewresearch.org/internet/2018/05/31/teens-social-media-technology-2018

Barnwell, P. (2016, April 27). Do smartphones have a place in the classroom? *The Atlantic*. https://www.theatlantic.com/education/archive/2016/04/do-smartphones-have-a-place-in-the-classroom/480231

Basen, I. (2012, December 19). *Breaking down the wall*. Center for Journalism Ethics. ethics.journalism.wisc.edu/2012/12/19/breaking-down-the-wall

Bell, B. (2014, June 29). Aww-some animals: Why do baby animals melt our hearts? *BBC News*. bbc.com/news/uk-england-28036667

Biden, J. R. (2021, January 21). *Inaugural address by President Joseph R. Biden, Jr.* The White House. whitehouse.gov/briefing-room/speeches-remarks/2021/01/20/inaugural-address-by-president-joseph-r-biden-jr

Blakeslee, S. (2004, Fall). The CRAAP test. *LOEX Quarterly. 31*(3), Article 4. https://commons.emich.edu/loexquarterly/vol31/iss3/4

Burton, N. (2012, May 23). Our hierarchy of needs. *Psychology Today*. https://www.psychologytoday.com/us/blog/hide-and-seek/201205/our-hierarchy-needs

CASEL (2020). *SEL: What are the core competence areas and where are they promoted?* Collaborative for Academic, Social, Emotional Learning (CASEL). casel.org/what-is-sel

Center for Media, Data and Society (2020, May 26). *How misinformation became a profitable business in Eastern Europe.* https://cmds.ceu.edu/article/2020-05-26/how-misinformation-became-profitable-business-eastern-europe

Denton, J. (2018, October 25). An information scientist talks media literacy, political memes, and the value of librarians. *Pacific Standard.* https://psmag.com/news/an-information-scientist-talks-media-literacy-political-memes-and-the-value-of-librarians

Dhabhar, F. S. (2018, April). The short-term stress response—Mother nature's mechanism for enhancing protection and performance under conditions of threat, challenge, and opportunity. *Frontiers in Neuroendocrinology, 49,* 175–192. https://www.sciencedirect.com/science/article/abs/pii/S0091302218300293

DiCamillo, K. (2021). *Stories connect us.* Candlewick Press. https://www.katedicamillostoriesconnectus.com/storiesconnectus

Everett, C. C. (2017, July 22). *Developing identity and empathy through independent reading* [Workshop]. 2017 Scholastic Reading Summit, Seattle, WA, United States.

Fifer, J. (2017, August 14). *By the numbers: American youth increasingly exposed to extremist messages online, Virginia Tech expert says.* VA Tech Daily. https://vtnews.vt.edu/articles/2017/08/unirel-online-extremism-hawdon.html

Gibson, C. (2019, September 17). 'Do you have teenage sons? Listen up.' How white supremacists are recruiting boys online. *The Washington Post.* https://www.washingtonpost.com/lifestyle/on-parenting/do-you-have-white-teenage-sons-listen-up-how-white-supremacists-are-recruiting-boys-online/2019/09/17/f081e806-d3d5-11e9-9343-40db57cf6abd_story.html

Gladwell, M. (2019). *Talking to strangers: What we should know about the people we don't know.* Little, Brown & Co.

GSMA Intelligence (2021). *Global mobile data sets.* https://www.gsmaintelligence.com/data

Gorman, A. (2021). *The hill we climb. An inaugural poem for the country.* Viking Books.

Grieco, E. (2020, February 14). *Fast facts about the newspaper industry's financial struggles as McClatchy files for bankruptcy.* Pew Research Center. https://www.pewresearch.org/fact-tank/2020/02/14/fast-facts-about-the-newspaper-industrys-financial-struggles

Gruber, M. J., Gelman, B. D., & Ranganath, C. (2014, October 2). States of curiosity modulate hippocampus-dependent learning via the dopaminergic circuit. *Neuron. 84*(2), 486–496. https://www.cell.com/neuron/fulltext/S0896-6273(14)00804-6

Haughney, C. (2013, December 29). Time Inc. is preparing to head out on its own. *The New York Times*. https://www.nytimes.com/2013/12/30/business/media/time-inc-is-preparing-to-head-out-on-its-own.html?pagewanted=all&_r=1&

Hoefler, K., & Luyken, C. (2020). *Nothing in common*. Houghton Mifflin Harcourt.

Hogenboom, M. (2016, January 26). We have known that Earth is round for over 2,000 years. *BBC News*. http://www.bbc.com/earth/story/20160126-how-we-know-earth-is-round

Kamenetz, A. (2017, October 31). *Learning to spot fake news: Start with a gut check*. NPR. https://www.npr.org/sections/ed/2017/10/31/559571970/learning-to-spot-fake-news-start-with-a-gut-check

Kiernan, L. (2017, December 29). *Calculating the work behind our work*. ProPublica. https://www.propublica.org/article/calculating-the-work-behind-our-work

Lewis, A. [@andlewis]. (2010, September 13). *If you're not paying for it, you're not the customer; you're the product being sold* [Tweet]. Twitter. https://twitter.com/andlewis/status/24380177712?lang=en

Long Island Exploratorium (2020). *Virtual programs guide*. https://longislandexplorium.org/virtual-programs

May, R. (1981). *Freedom and destiny*. W. W. Norton & Company.

MacFarquhar, N. (2019, November 23). Nazi symbols and racist memes: Combating school intolerance. *The New York Times*. https://www.nytimes.com/2019/11/23/us/extremism-schools-white-supremacy.html

Maslow, A. H. (1943). A theory of human motivation. *Psychological Review, 50*(4), 370–396. https://doi.apa.org/doiLanding?doi=10.1037%2Fh0054346

McFadden, C. (2020, July 2). *A chronological history of social media*. Interesting Engineering. https://interestingengineering.com/a-chronological-history-of-social-media

McSpadden, K. (2015, May 14). You now have a shorter attention span than a goldfish. *Time*. time.com/3858309/attention-spans-goldfish

Metz, C. (2020, October 29). Twitter bots poised to spread disinformation before election. *The New York Times*. https://www.nytimes.com/2020/10/29/technology/twitter-bots-poised-to-spread-disinformation-before-election.html

Meyer, R. (2018, March 8). The grim conclusions of the largest-ever study of fake news. *The Atlantic*. https://www.theatlantic.com/technology/archive/2018/03/largest-study-ever-fake-news-mit-twitter/555104

Montessori, M. (1995). *The absorbent mind*. Henry Holt and Company.

Muhtaris, K., & Ziemke, K. (2019). *Read the world: Rethinking literacy for empathy and action in a digital age*. Heinemann Press.

Nayeri, D. (2020, August 25). *Everything sad is untrue*. Levine Querido Books.

Oetting, J. (2017, July 28). *10 effective emotional triggers that make people buy* [Infographic]. HubSpot. https://blog.hubspot.com/agency/emotional-triggers-infographic

O'Sullivan, D. (2019). *When seeing is no longer believing: Inside the Pentagon's race against deepfake videos.* CNN Business. https://www.cnn.com/interactive/2019/01/business/pentagons-race-against-deepfakes/

O'Toole, C. (2017, July 16). You're not the customer; you're the product. Quote Investigator. https://quoteinvestigator.com/2017/07/16/product/

Pariser, E. (2011, March). *Beware online 'filter bubbles'* [Video]. TED Conferences. https://www.ted.com/talks/eli_pariser_beware_online_filter_bubbles?language=en

Pesce, M. (2020, November 23). Why the web spreads information and misinformation equally well. *IEEE Spectrum.* https://spectrum.ieee.org/computing/software/why-the-web-spreads-information-and-misinformation-equally-well.amp.html

Pew Research Center. (2021, April 7). *Internet/broadband fact sheet.* https://www.pewresearch.org/internet/fact-sheet/internet-broadband

Rhodes, M. (2017, October 2). *When children begin to lie, there's actually a positive takeaway.* NPR. https://www.npr.org/sections/13.7/2017/10/02/552860553/when-children-begin-to-lie-theres-actually-a-positive-takeaway

Rideout, V., & Robb, M. B. (2019). *The Common Sense census: Media use by tweens and teens, 2019.* Common Sense Media. https://www.commonsensemedia.org/sites/default/files/uploads/research/2019-census-8-to-18-key-findings-updated.pdf

Ringov, D. (2020, July 10). Education in the age of fake news, distraction, and vanity. *Forbes.* https://www.forbes.com/sites/esade/2020/07/10/education-in-the-age-of-fake-news-distraction-and-vanity/?sh=16d9860a28d8

Rose-Stockwell, T. (2017, July 14). *This is how your fear and outrage are being sold for profit.* Medium. https://tobiasrose.medium.com/the-enemy-in-our-feeds-e86511488de

Rushkoff, D. (2020, January 22). *All media connect us before they tear us apart.* Team Human. https://medium.com/team-human/all-media-connect-us-before-they-tear-us-apart-9f333c0c7b2f

Saldanha, N. (2019, November 19). In 2018, an 8-year-old made $22 million on YouTube. No wonder kids want to be influencers. *Fast Company.* https://www.fastcompany.com/90432765/why-do-kids-want-to-be-influencers

Sehl, K. (2019, April 10). *All the different ways to calculate engagement rate (free calculator).* Hootsuite. https://blog.hootsuite.com/calculate-engagement-rate

Sivek, S. C. (2018, October 2). Both facts and feelings: Emotion and news literacy. *Journal of Media Literacy Education. 10*(2), 123–138. https://digitalcommons.uri.edu/cgi/viewcontent.cgi?article=1355&context=jmle

Smith, A., & Banic, B. (2016, December 9). *Fake news: How a partying Macedonian teen earns thousands publishing lies.* NBC News. https://www.nbcnews.com/news/world/fake-news-how-partying-macedonian-teen-earns-thousands-publishing-lies-n692451

Sontag, S. (2011). *On photography*. Farrar, Straus and Giroux.

Spector, N. (2017, December 16). *'Headline stress disorder': How to cope with the anxiety caused by the 24/7 news cycle*. NBC News. https://www.nbcnews.com/better/health/what-headline-stress-disorder-do-you-have-it-ncna830141

Starbird, K. (2019, July 24). Disinformation's spread: Bots, trolls and all of us. *Nature*. https://www.nature.com/articles/d41586-019-02235-x

Sukovic, S. (2016, September 15). *What exactly is transliteracy?* SciTech Connect. http://scitechconnect.elsevier.com/what-exactly-is-transliteracy

Sundar, S. S. (2016, December 7). *Why do we fall for fake news?* The Conversation. https://theconversation.com/why-do-we-fall-for-fake-news-69829

Torre, J. B., & Lieberman, M. D. (2018, March 20). Putting feelings into words: Affect labeling as implicit emotion regulation. *Emotion Review. 10*(2), 116–124. https://doi.org/10.1177/1754073917742706

Vosoughi, S., Roy, D., & Aral, S. (2018, March 9). The spread of true and false news online. *Science. 359*(6380), 1146–1151. science.sciencemag.org/content/359/6380/1146

Waldman, K. (2016, November 21). *The one-star blitz on Megyn Kelly's book and the political weaponization of Amazon blurbs*. Slate. https://slate.com/culture/2016/11/how-fringe-groups-are-turning-one-star-amazon-reviews-into-political-speech.html

Walker, M. (2019, November 19). *Americans favor mobile devices over desktops and laptops for getting news*. Pew Research Center. https://www.pewresearch.org/fact-tank/2019/11/19/americans-favor-mobile-devices-over-desktops-and-laptops-for-getting-news

Wardle, C., & Derakhshan, H. (2017, September 27). *Information disorder: Toward an interdisciplinary framework for research and policy making*. Council of Europe. https://rm.coe.int/information-disorder-toward-an-interdisciplinary-framework-for-researc/168076277c

Wheatley, M. (2017). *Who do we choose to be?: Facing reality, claiming leadership, restoring sanity*. Berrett-Koehler Publishers.

WHO, UN, UNICEF, UNDP, UNESCO, UNAIDS, ITU, UN Global Pulse, & IFRC. (2020, September 23). *Managing the COVID-19 infodemic: Promoting healthy behaviours and mitigating the harm from misinformation and disinformation*. World Health Organization. https://www.who.int/news/item/23-09-2020-managing-the-covid-19-infodemic-promoting-healthy-behaviours-and-mitigating-the-harm-from-misinformation-and-disinformation

WHO & UNICEF (2010). *WHO/UNICEF joint monitoring report 2010: Progress on sanitation and drinking water—fast facts*. World Health Organization. https://www.who.int/docs/default-source/wash-documents/wash-coverage/jmp/jmp2010-fast-facts.pdf?sfvrsn=b352b475_2

Wineburg, S., & McGrew, S. (2017, October 6). *Lateral reading: Reading less and learning more when evaluating digital information.* https://dx.doi.org/10.2139/ssrn.3048994

Wineburg, S. [@samwineburg]. (2019, November 3). *What does web savvy have to do with historical thinking? Lots. Here's a meme that came across one of my* [Tweet]. Twitter. https://twitter.com/samwineburg/status/1191065078021255168?s=20

Yuhas, D. (2014, October 2). Curiosity prepares the brain for better learning. *Scientific American.* https://www.scientificamerican.com/article/curiosity-prepares-the-brain-for-better-learning

Index